BAI
for the
HURRIED WOMAN

Time Management Strategies

by

DAWN ULMER

ISBN-13: 978-1546586418

Dedication

To each woman who strives to live a balanced
life which
brings glory to God.

"By wisdom a house is built,
And by understanding it is established;
By knowledge the rooms are filled
with all precious and pleasant riches."
Proverbs 24:3-4

CONTENTS

A PERSONAL WORD

When did it begin, I wondered? Looking back, I now realize that I was born with a certain personality type which means I too easily fall into a hurried lifestyle.

I believe I first noticed my hurried tendencies when I was in college taking classes toward a Bachelor of Science degree in nursing. There was always something to memorize, study, and papers to write. Plus I worked in a hospital on weekends.

Newly married, I settled into my new life. Fast forward about eight years when my son was six and I began to pick up speed. I was working part-time and my hurried ways were brought to my attention by my son's second grade teacher as she described him as "always busy, hurrying on to do the next project". I saw her describing ME. I was always hurrying headed toward burn out. I decided to stop working outside the home and work from home which took tremendous pressure off. I sold advertising and with my profits bought a home-based business creating custom made bridal veils and hats. For the next 9 years I kept busy but at a sane pace.

When my son was 15, I found out that I was pregnant with my daughter. With a baby, it was impossible to keep my business so I sold it. As she turned five and I began the long journey of homeschooling her, I noticed that she had begun to stutter. There are many reasons why stuttering takes place, but I began evaluating to see if I was doing anything to cause it. Sure enough, my continual words of, "Hurry up!" echoed through the house. We had places to go and things to do – the bookmobile, play group, books to read, time outside.... It was time again to dial it back and go at a more sane pace. The stuttering disappeared completely.

I have recently retired and suddenly find that I am becoming a hurried woman once again. I find myself saying, "I don't know when I found time to work!". It was time to once again pick up the principles in this book that I'd used as circumstances changed throughout my life. I also wanted to put these principles in book form to share with others.

Who do I acknowledge? GOD! By His indwelling Holy Spirit, He has helped me through the years to keep moving in a good direction as a woman…and gently stopped me when I have tended toward becoming a Hurried Woman. He is the one who created balance in each of my days as I listened to His wisdom in how to walk through the seasons of my life. He knows me because He created me. When I acknowledge His ownership of me and listen, He directs me daily.

YES, it is possible to reach a good balance in our ever-changing lives. I hope this book and the ideas presented here will be of help to you.

"For You, God, created my inmost being;
You knit me together in my mother's womb.
I praise You because I am fearfully and wonderfully made. Your works are wonderful,
I know that full well."
Psalm 139:13-14

"In all your ways acknowledge Him,
And He will direct your paths."
Proverbs 3:6

CHAPTER 1

STEP OFF THE MERRY-GO-ROUND

***Why Be Concerned About A Hurried Lifestyle?**
***Quiz: How Hurried Are You?**
***Are You Juggling or Balancing Your Life?**
***Your Home's Atmosphere**
***Eleven Reasons Why We Hurry**
***Keep a Time Log**
***Say NO to Procrastination**

"If any of you lacks wisdom, you should ask God, who gives generously to all without finding fault, and it will be given to you."

James 1:5

As we all know, a merry-go-round can be a pleasant experience. It can also become a nightmare if it just goes round and round, never stopping and YOU CAN'T GET OFF!

Step off the merry-go-round! That is what we as women need to do periodically to gain perspective and to keep a clear view in our lives. We need to prayerfully and thoughtfully re-evaluate who we are, where we've been, where we are now and where we want to go in future days and years.

Notice the term *rat race* wasn't used. Women are involved in doing GOOD – nurturing their family, being a diligent employee and being involved in their community and place of worship. Thus, the term merry-go-round was used.

No matter how good our lives are, however, we need to periodically re-evaluate them. Reading this book slowly and thoughtfully in terms of YOUR life is one way of stepping back to get a clearer perspective and to see where you are going. Ponder the words. Read at a leisurely pace. Take time to think in depth about what is said. The rewards will be well worth the time spent.

Why Be Concerned About a Hurried Lifestyle?

"Be careful, or your hearts will be weighed down with … the anxieties of life, and that day will close on you suddenly like a trap."
Luke 21:34

Have you ever felt at the point of burnout? I have, a couple of times, and knew that I was in trouble if I didn't make some changes. I don't ever want to go there again.

Why should YOU be concerned? Our society today has definitely increased in speed. We have meals which almost cook themselves, fast food restaurants, express lanes in the grocery store, quick craft patterns for that quick gift and computers and devices which are valued for their speed. No longer do we take the time to send a handwritten note or even have a friendly chat on the phone, we text or email our thoughts, sometimes not even in full sentences.

Researchers, as stated in *The Hurrier I Go* by Bonnie Wheeler, have found that women today work MORE hours per week than our grandmothers did. Think about it.

Our homes have become larger as we've added family rooms, more bedrooms, huge closets and an office. We have more area to care for and, correspondingly, more possessions fill the space to dust, polish, wash and keep in order. Not only do we work more inside the home, but often we work outside the home, too.

Due to this increased workload (real or perceived), our stress levels go higher and higher until that stress begins to manifest itself in our body with health issues, infections, heart issues, high blood sugar, a compromised immune system and burnout - we are affected head to toe, inwardly and outwardly.

Adding a new baby to a household increases the workload by at least 40% according to Elise Arndt in "A Mother's Time".

Lately we have been led to believe that we can go through pregnancy, delivery of a baby and a return to work without skipping a beat. Are 'they' CRAZY? It takes tremendous energy for a woman's body to nourish new life within, to go through labor and delivery and to learn how to mother and raise a child. Even if a woman is married and has a spouse, her work load is tremendous. For single women it can be back breaking.

The job of mothering is intense for at least 18 years. My thoughts are that if a baby increases the work load by 40%, a toddler must increase it by 80% and a teenager by 160%. Why does it take more work to successfully raise a teenager? Think about it. A toddler, pre-schooler and baby are usually at home with you and under your watchful eye. When a child becomes a teen and older, they are gone from home many hours a day, have their own friends, are on social media, texting, wanting to attend parties, learning to drive, getting that first job. A parent's job is NEVER done even when that child matures and moves out on their own. They still need a loving heart and listening ear.

We are all hurried women at one time or another. We fix a quick dinner so we can run out the door to an evening meeting. We rush ourselves and our children out the door to soccer practice, ballet, trumpet lessons and hockey games. Our project at work was due yesterday. We find that a *once in a while* hurried day becomes a part of our character and we become what we never intended to be – a HURRIED WOMAN.

According to the author of the book, *We Are Driven - The Compulsive Behavior America Applauds* by Minirth and Meier, busyness can become a chronic problem…it does not go away unless we deal with the deeper causes. It is also progressive and, over time, the busyness will pick up speed and momentum. It will only get WORSE. That's scary! WHAT CAN WE DO?

Let's find out if YOU have a problem with a hurried lifestyle by completing the **How Hurried Are YOU? Quiz**.

How Hurried Are YOU?

Circle the number which most applies to you:

1 Never 2 Sometimes 3 Always

1. Do you rush through your day from project to project?

1 2 3

2. Do you find yourself unable to relax and enjoy a day off?

1 2 3

3. Do you feel you don't have enough time in the day to get everything completed?

1 2 3

4. Does your mind race ahead to think about what you should do next?

1 2 3

5. Does your body feel tense?

1 2 3

6. Do you see yourself as over-committed and with too many areas of responsibility?

1 2 3

7. Do you find you are impatient while you wait in line?

1 2 3

8. Do you try to do more than one thing at a time?

1 2 3

9. Do you find yourself unable to take, relax and enjoy a vacation?

1 2 3

10. Do you find yourself impatient with others who are slower than you are?

1 2 3

11. Are you competitive at work and at recreational pursuits?

1 2 3

Total your score and write the number here: _____

If you scored 11-15 you are doing well. Good job!
If you scored 16-20 be careful! Read on.
If you scored 21-33 you are HURRIED! Read on.

In light of the findings of this quiz, it is important to keep in mind the **Empty Hands Principle** (I invented this for myself). I must not fill my hands so full that I don't have room for one more thing in them. For example, if a child needs extra attention, is there room in my hands to just sit, read some books together and snuggle? If God gives me a task to do which isn't on my schedule, do I have time to do it or are my hands too full? Let's always leave some space each day for the unexpected!

"If we really have too much to do, there are some items on the agenda which God did not put there. Let us submit the list to Him and ask Him to indicate which items we must delete. There is always time to do the will of God. If we are too busy to do that, we are too busy."

– Elisabeth Elliot

If you want to slow your pace, solutions must be used diligently and consistently in order to remedy each area you identify as hurried and full of stress. Here are eleven tips to help you slow down:

1. If you rush from project to project, stop when one project is completed. Take a deep breath and consider if and when you should move to your next project on your to do list.

2. If you have difficulty relaxing on your days off and instead use your day off to play catch-up, make a list of fun, relaxing and rejuvenating activities that would bring you pleasure. Then enjoy your day!

3. If you think that your day is too packed to complete everything, perhaps it is. Review your calendar, set priorities and then do the most important first.

4. If your mind is racing ahead then you aren't truly in the present. What are you missing now? Pull yourself back to the present by focusing on what is happening NOW.

5. A tense body is a signal that all is not well. Breathe deeply, relax and slow down.

6. If you see yourself as over-committed, perhaps you are. Begin to lighten the load by learning to say NO – we will discuss this more later.

7. Use the time waiting in line to become more aware of what is happening around you. You are being delayed for a reason. Be thankful for the pause.

8. Are you doing more than one thing at a time? We cook dinner, talk on the phone, feed the baby and create the latest novel in our heads – all at once. Why? Doing one thing at a time and enjoying each can slow our pace.

9. Do you have difficulty taking, relaxing during and enjoying a vacation? Instead of using your vacation to do more work or even running to and fro seeking fun, purposefully carve out some quiet spaces of time to be renewed and rejuvenated.

10. Are you impatient with others? Spend some time with toddlers and the elderly. They can teach us that speed isn't as important as we think. They value what is important -- hugs, reading a book together and a slow walk around the block.

11. Teamwork is healthier than a competitive spirit. Let's leave competitiveness on the tennis court and begin practicing teamwork where it counts – at home and on the job.

Are You Juggling or Balancing Your Life?

"This is what the Lord says—
your Redeemer, the Holy One of Israel:
'am the Lord your God,
who teaches you what is best for you,
who directs you in the way you should go."
Isaiah 48:17

There is a huge difference between juggling and balancing life's responsibilities. Let's define the two terms:

Juggling the responsibilities and joys of our lives requires perfect timing. Our hands are full. Every moment is packed. Then your child becomes ill or there is a problem at work. All comes crashing down around you. The perfect juggling act has become a disaster area.

Balancing the responsibilities and joys of our lives, however, requires timing and flexibility. Our hands are empty enough to allow for the emergency, the interruption and the hundreds of circumstances that can change our direction.

Please ask yourself: Are you juggling or balancing your life?

Often, leaving empty spaces within the day means we are available for something good that God may have planned for you. If every minute of every day is jam packed, it's time to create some availability. Something wonderful may happen!

Attaining and maintaining a balanced life should be our goal. If we allow God to direct us, He will!

Your Home's Atmosphere

"For you were once darkness, but now you are light in the Lord. Live as children of light (for the fruit of the light consists in all goodness, righteousness and truth)."

Ephesians 5:8-9

We all know that the woman helps set the tone of the home. A woman at peace and well organized will have a home which reflects her character. A hurried, frazzled woman will affect everyone and everything around her in a negative manner.

Caution is needed! Our children not only become out of sorts because of a frazzled and hurried home life, they also can perceive our hurry as rejection. As we zip around the kitchen, upstairs, downstairs and out the door, our children aren't sure what we said, where we went or what we are doing. They may feel rejected.

Listen to what the famous author Pearl S. Buck has to say about this in her book, *To My Daughters, With Love*:

> "Sweet tempered children grow easily in a pleasantly planned and well-ordered home. Irritable children and impatient, unhappy adults are the result…of the atmosphere in an unpleasant and disorderly home."

Often, because we are hurried, we allow and even encourage our children to live hurried lives. We overload them with school, soccer, church meetings, ballet and overnight sleep-overs.

David Elkins in his book *The Hurried Child* states: "restlessness, irritability, inability to concentrate and low mood is perhaps the most pervasive immediate response children exhibit to the stress of hurrying."

Are you allowing and encouraging a hurried lifestyle in your home and with your children?

How careful we must be!

Eleven Reasons Why We Hurry

Why do we hurry? Have you ever thought about it? Below are eleven possible reasons:

1. **Did you hear "Well done" ?**
   Many of us were raised by parents who were not taught to tell us "Well done". If we received a B on a report card, we weren't told how proud they were of us, we were challenged to strive for the A. Here we are 20, 30, 50 years later and we find ourselves hurrying and scurrying around still trying to earn that "Well done".

2. **Are you driven?**
   Many women feel good about themselves only through their accomplishments. They are not content with who they are as a

person so they strive to climb the career ladder at work, head as many community committees as they can or volunteer for a multitude of responsibilities at their place of worship. They are **driven** to accomplish more and more so that they can feel better about themselves.

3. Are you preoccupied with symbols of accomplishment?

Many women are pre-occupied with symbols of their and/or their spouse's accomplishments. They want a bigger house, more job recognition, a nicer car and fancier furnishings. There is nothing wrong with trying to better ourselves and our circumstances. Driven women, however, tend to go overboard and become preoccupied with the symbols of their accomplishments, always needing more.

4. Are you a stressaholic?

Adrenalin in our body is a socially acceptable drug. A stressaholic thinks she must finish one more thing and then she can relax. She then goes on, however, to the next project without a break. She believes that she must be constantly productive and continues to push herself day after day seeking perfection in herself and in others. She can't stop. She is hooked on a high level of adrenalin – she is addicted to stress.

5. **Are you trying to look important?**
   As we hurry and scurry and puff our way through our busyness, others stand back and think, "How important she must be, look how FAST she's going!" Even if no one is watching, the hurried woman's imaginary audience is cheering her on and she responds by going faster to please them.

6. **Are you trying to make yourself indispensable?**
   By having the household, work projects, and committees depend totally on you, subtly you are striving to gain power by making yourself indispensable. Also, sometimes we have friends who take, take, take but never give back to you. Are you unavailable to those who mean the most to you because you've made yourself indispensable to some who want to *use* you?

7. **Are you trying to avoid responsibilities?**
   By being too busy, unwanted responsibilities and unpleasant tasks are pushed into the background. Many women would rather be President of the Society to Preserve Societies than to quietly, day in and day out, care for an ailing elderly parent.

8. **Are you avoiding new experiences or change?**
   By being too busy, we can avoid new experiences and resist change. It is much easier to be busy doing familiar tasks than to learn new skills or have new expcriences. There are classes to take, new books to read, new skills to learn and new people to meet. Our busyness can prevent the addition of new experiences in our lives.

9. **Are you avoiding everyday home responsibilities?**
   By being too busy, we can shirk our home responsibilities of caring for our families. Meal preparation, laundry or cleaning isn't done or done well. It is easier and more fun to do the *flashy* than the seemingly mundane.

10. **Are you making yourself unavailable?**
   By being too busy we can hedge ourselves in with busyness so that we are unavailable to those around us. It takes far less time and energy to have a surface relationship with someone than it does to establish a loving, caring relationship which gains depth through the years. (More on that later.)

11. Are you trying to ease guilt?

By being too busy, we can try to ease some of the guilt we feel because we sense that our life is too easy. Every day we are bombarded with the latest tragedies in our world – bombings, train derailments, deadly storms…. In comparison, our corner of the world seems quite plush.

Do you see yourself in any of these reasons why YOU hurry?

Keep a Time Log

"You make known to me the path of life;
You will fill me with joy in Your presence,
with eternal pleasures at Your right hand."
Psalm 16:11

We've discussed stepping off the merry-go-round and that if we don't change our hurried lifestyle, the problem becomes chronic which gets worse over time. The Hurried Woman Quiz pinpointed some possible problem areas. We've discussed whether we are juggling or balancing our lives and we've discussed the eleven reasons why we hurry.

Let's turn our attention deeper now to even more specifics.

When we find ourselves picking up speed and the stress begins to build, that's a perfect opportunity to take a longer look at what is happening in our lives. One excellent way to discover how we use our time is by keeping a time log, whether on paper or online. We each have 24 hours per day and, as busy women, we want to use each God-given moment wisely.

You say there is no time to keep a time log? That's precisely the point! When we deny ourselves the time it takes to make our lives better for ourselves and for those whom we love, then our priorities need to be rearranged. A time log can be of great value.

Do something just for yourself this week. Either purchase a small, perky-looking notebook you can carry with you or set up something with one of the many apps available to help you keep a log. For seven days, write down how you spend your time for each of the 24 hours. Remember, you are doing this for yourself so do it as completely and accurately as possible.

At the end of seven days, take some quiet time to look over your time log entries. Ask yourself the following questions:

- Am I trying to fit 36 hours worth of work into 24 hours?

- Do I have time to take care of household necessities or am I too busy in other areas?

- How many hours did I spend at work this week? (Make sure to include the time you spent with work you took home at night and on weekends, including phone calls.)

- Does my family get the best hours of my day or only the leftovers?

- Is unnecessary time on the phone or texting (personal or business use) chewing up precious minutes?

- Are there spaces in my day which allow me time to think ahead and to plan for the next day, the next week?

- Do I allow any time for myself each day to relax and unwind?

- Do I have one day per week I can use to rest, relax and be rejuvenated?

- Am I allowing myself enough time to get a full night's sleep so I awake refreshed?

How does your time log look?

Say No to Procrastination

– Reasons Why We Procrastinate
– Seven Tips to Get the Job Done
– How to Keep Yourself Motivated

"…what does the Lord your God ask of you but to fear the Lord your God, to walk in obedience to Him, to love Him, to serve the Lord your God with all your heart and with all your soul, and to observe the Lord's commands and decrees that I am giving you today for your own good?"
Deuteronomy 10:12-13

What does procrastination have to do with a hurried lifestyle? Isn't procrastination slowing way down so that things don't get done? That's part of it. The other part of it is the aftermath of procrastinations - **hurrying** to get done what needed to be done in the first place.

Let me give you some examples: Your tooth has been bothering you for weeks but you keep putting off that call to the dentist. There is a slight leak in the dining room ceiling but you hope it was a one time problem and that the stain will fade with time. The car has a strange knocking sound coming from under the hood but you just don't want to take the time to have it checked out. Maybe it will go away. We procrastinate – put off until tomorrow what we should do today…now. Then tomorrow we don't do it either.

All of us procrastinate at one time or another. Procrastination, however, becomes a problem when we find ourselves procrastinating over too many things over too long a period of time. Then procrastination insidiously invades our characters and we paralyze ourselves with our inactivity.

Eventually we begin to notice that it is taking more time to evade a task than it does to actually do it. All of our *to-dos* begin to pile up. Then we notice ourselves becoming irritable, anxious and frustrated. We begin to lose our tempers and hate ourselves for how we are acting – all because we keep putting off doing something we know we should have done yesterday.

Reasons Why We Procrastinate

We procrastinate for a variety of reasons, some of which may be the following:

* We'd rather be doing something else.
* We magnify the time it takes to complete a task.

* We feel overwhelmed with too much to do.
* We hope someone else will do the job if we don't.
* We want to wait until we can do the job more thoroughly and perfectly.
* We don't *feel* like doing the project.
* We don't know where to begin and sometimes don't want to admit that we don't know how to do part or all of the job.
* We overcommit ourselves.
* We fear failure.
* If truth be told, sometimes we just don't want to do the job.

When we determine why we procrastinate on a chore, job or project, then we can begin to deal with the problem. Basically, the solution to any procrastination problem is: **DO IT NOW**!

Do you know why YOU procrastinate?

Seven Tips to Get the Job Done

1. Begin immediately. Don't give yourself even one second to think about it, make excuses or try to talk your way around it. Do it now!

2. Set a deadline. Decide when you want the task completed, then do it!

3. Make time for the task. Set aside a reasonable block of time for the task, then do it!

4. Do the worst part first. When the worst job or worst portion of the job is out of the way, all else looks easy, even inviting. Do it!

5. Break a major task into small steps. Estimate the time needed to complete each step, then do it!

6. Be accountable. Ask a friend or co-worker to help keep you accountable for what must be done. Then do it!

7. Take advantage of free moments. Perhaps a meeting has been canceled or an appointment has been postponed. Redeem the time and do it!

How to Keep Yourself Motivated

* **Work within your energy level.** Determine at what time of day or night you do your best work. Then fit your tasks into that time frame.

* **Convert work into minutes.** Often we think a job will take longer than it actually does. If we see a job in terms of minutes, we see the job as manageable.

* **Compete with yourself.** If it took you 20 minutes last time to do a task, streamline the process and beat the time.

* **Find a simpler way.** If a task is too involved, try eliminating some aspects and combining the work. For example, it is easier to water one planter full of plants than ten plants spread throughout the house.

* **Revise your master to-do list periodically.** Keep your priorities on track knowing what tasks need to be done first.

* **Establish a schedule.** If you decide that the laundry is to be done on Mondays and Thursdays, there is no room for debate. Stick to your established schedule (within reason and if possible).

* **Make your working environment more pleasant.** Treat yourself to a vase of fresh flowers, a new plant, better lighting, a new table covering. Doing the task can become a pleasure.

* **Don't get sidetracked.** There are so many distractions -- our phones, a text message comes in, emails which must be answered.... Turn everything **off** as you block out some time to get things done...and notice how much you accomplish.

* **Reward yourself.** If you are successful in meeting your goal, give yourself a reward. Take a walk, call a friend, go out to lunch.... Do it now!

CHAPTER 2

SIMPLIFY YOUR LIFE

***Simplify Your Activities**
***Simplify Your Relationships**
***Simplify Your Possessions**

"Don't copy the behavior and customs of this world, but let God transform you into a new person by changing the way you think. Then you will learn to know God's will for you, which is good and pleasing and perfect."
Romans 12:2

We women have been told that we can *have it all.* Then we found that we were overwhelmed because we were expected to *do it all* in order to have it all. Now we are seeing that we can live more satisfying lives by intentional voluntary simplicity.

Voluntary simplicity seems to be a direct outgrowth of the choices women have had to make. When we learned that it wasn't enough to *just* be single or a career woman or a wife and a mother, we became exhausted trying to be a perfect wife, perfect mother AND perfect career woman.

We were also expected to take classes or learn new skills so that we could continue marching up the career ladder. What next, we wondered.... Our days were already too full.

When we realize that we don't have to fit into a certain mold that society expects, we can question where we are and where we are going. We don't have to be everything to everybody; we can listen to our hearts.

When we listen to our hearts, some of us may decide to work outside the home but for a limited number of hours so that we can be home for our families and home for ourselves. Some of us may decide to stop the march up the career ladder since the cost is too great to ourselves and to those we love if we keep climbing. Some of us may head home and be perfectly content and flourish as stay-at-home wives and mothers. We have begun to see the importance of being who God created us to be and doing what He wants us to do. That is more important than accumulating money, things and prestige.

"Sometimes money costs too much," states Annie Chapman in her book *Smart Women Keep It Simple.* Voluntary simplicity can and should extend to all areas of our lives -- our activities, our relationships and our possessions.

SIMPLIFY YOUR ACTIVITIES

– Say No to the Tyranny of the Urgent
– The Dangers of Not saying No and Burnout
– Reasons Why We Don't Say No
– How to Say No

In order to simplify your life, you must learn to say **NO.** Most of us, however, have a problem saying NO to the requests and demands which bombard us. Toddlers say it quite easily, I wonder why we women don't use NO more often?
"A superwoman is not a woman who can do anything but a woman who avoids doing too much," states Shirley Conran in *Superwoman.*

Say NO to the Tyranny of the Urgent

"Do not be afraid! Don't be discouraged by this mighty army, for the battle is not yours, but God's."
II Chronicles 20:15b

The tyranny of the urgent can be as simple as your phone ringing all day and all night or texts arriving non-stop while interrupting what you are doing:
driving home from work
cooking dinner
eating dinner with your family
spending quality time with your child
or trying to sleep
Please pause to think through what is happening. Our device-oriented society only points to the fact that

interruptions are now a part of our culture. It used to be a knock at the door from a neighbor, now it is people and even robots calling to interrupt what you should be doing.

Prayerfully consider the importance of that interruption and then you can decide what to do about it:

Control the interruption.
Put your device on mute until after you have accomplished what you need to do that day, that minute. Put a peep hole in your door and refuse to answer it unless you know who is coming to visit. *You* be in control of your life, not devices or other people. If a child continually interrupts you, find a diversion for them until you have completed your task.

Eliminate the interruption.
Don't answer the door, don't answer your phone, don't text. You can get back to them…or not. For robots calling, get put on a Do Not Call List.

We *must* keep our lives as streamlined as possible because it is a busy world. Your time and energy are of utmost importance and need to be guarded.

The Dangers of Not Saying No

"And all his busy rushing ends in NOTHING."
Psalm 39:6

The refusal to say NO creates stress in a woman's life! The terms *stress* and *burnout* were relatively unknown in our mothers' and grandmothers' times. Women today, however, have so many more choices than in the past. When we don't say NO, we become overwhelmed by doing too much and by having too much.

As we all know, stress takes its toll physically, spiritually, psychologically and emotionally by sapping our energy – one of our most precious resources. As humans, we have only so much energy. When demands on our energy surpass the amount of energy we have, we suffer! As we increase in age from 20 to 80, we feel a decrease in physical energy even though our psychological, intellectual and spiritual energy may continue to abound. However, if we squander one type of energy, then energy across the span is affected. The result? We become stressed out and then burned out. We no longer enjoy life.

Have you ever visited the Land of Burnout? I did once and ever thereafter guard against going there again! It was a dark time. I didn't know what was wrong with me. I can remember thinking, "I'm hanging on by a thread!" I was doing all of the right things at home and at work – going above and beyond. Nothing I did helped - the stress of my life was still there and building.

Burnout doesn't suddenly happen. It happens as a result of too much stress over too long a period of time. It is a gradual wearing away of time and energy . What is the result? Life looks flat and uninteresting. There is no joy, even in the things you may have always enjoyed doing. You end up just going through the motions.

Signs of Impending Burnout

It's important to recognize these danger signs in our lives:
*Always being tired. No amount of rest or sleep helps.

* The immune system can be worn out – we can no longer fight something as common as the common cold, not to mention a serious illness.

* Thinking may not be as clear as it once was. There can be difficulty remembering and concentrating.

* Health issues may surface – heart palpitations, chest pain, abdominal pain, shortness of breath, dizziness, diabetes, headaches. Some symptoms may have medical reasons so it would be good to see a physician for a good baseline reading on your health. Make sure he or she knows how much stress you have been experiencing.

* Food doesn't taste good or you are overeating to pump up your energy level. Caution is needed here - energy drinks, caffeine and sugar are *not* a good habit to get into in order to get an energy boost.

* Anxiety – over everything, big and little – feeling overwhelmed.

* Anger and increased irritability – all of that suppressed stress begins to come out.

* Depression – there are many causes of depression so make sure your stressful lifestyle isn't one of the causes.

* Feeling cynical, detached, pessimistic and isolated --if this is unusual for you, take a look at your stress level.

* Lack of enjoyment in the simple pleasures of life – maybe you even begin to avoid life since none of it seems enjoyable.

* Feeling hopeless – that no matter what you do or how much you do, nothing makes a difference. What's the use?

* Feeling useless which leads to poor performance in the things you do and thus, lack of productivity. You are at a standstill.

CAUTION IS NEEDED IF YOU FIND YOURSELF CONSISTENTLY STRESSED LEADING TO ANY OF THE ABOVE.

Trust me, I know what each symptom feels like. Thankfully, as soon as I realized WHAT it was - a 'simple' case of too much stress over too long a period of time, I began to self correct the areas which needed correction Using the principles in this book, life began to look better and I began to feel better once again. I stopped being a victim of life but was victorious. That alone began to pull me out of burnout.

As I mentioned, it took only ONE time for me to visit the Land of Burnout to never want to return there again. I know that if I let my life run away with me, I'm headed there -- so I correct and correct until life looks sparkling again.

Let's remember – as we sprint through all of life's duties and responsibilities, items become a blur on our to do list. They become one more thing to cross out. We no longer derive joy from creating a home of peace with good books, good music and a vase of flowers on the table. Our refusal to say NO has robbed us of the joys of simple pleasures and of serving those whom we love.

When women refuse to say NO, our family, friends and co-workers suffer right along with us. What are the results?

*Our family members may feel unloved because time is not spent with them and the practical necessities of life are not present – a nutritious meal, a clean home or clean clothing.

*Neither are the children being trained to take over some of the responsibilities they need to learn to be successful adults.

*When we try to do it *all*, family members and co-workers do not have the opportunity to learn new skills and to practice them because *we* are doing them.

As we hurry and scurry about, others look at us and wonder, "Is *this* what it means to be a woman?" For our daughters, especially, we should strive to give a clear picture of all womanhood can be - the *best* of womanhood. We don't want to give the impression that being a woman means being frazzled, stressed and hurried.

Reasons Why We Don't say No

The reasons we don't say no are many and varied. Here are just a few:

1. We want to feel that our lives are worthwhile so we say YES, YES, YES.

If we aren't doing something outstanding, important and fantastic, we believe that we are worthless. Thus, we keep collecting more things to do -- we never say NO. It is no longer enough to be a woman, career person, wife and mother, now we must be a brain surgeon on the side to feel worthwhile.

2. We seek approval from others so we say YES when we long to say NO.

After all, we reason, who could possibly like me for just being me? We believe that we need to do something more so others approve of us and love us. Thus, we say YES, trying to do more, seeking love and approval.

3. We feel so responsible for everyone and everything.

We say YES and continue to accept responsibility for things that aren't ours to do and then we wonder why everyone else is sitting around doing nothing while we are scurrying around.

A quote from James Walker in *Smart Women Keep It Simple* will serve as a warning to women who tend to take over the responsibilities of the man in the home:

> "When a man's position is challenged or thwarted, he will retreat, giving less to the marriage. He may stop bringing his

> personality, his energy and his creativity home. A woman's natural tendency then is to assume the space that has been vacated by her husband. She becomes more than she should be in order to make up for his emotional absence and to restore the home to working order."
> Further, "She initiates conversation because 'he won't talk'. She takes over all the bill-paying because 'they'll turn out the lights'. What results is a functioning family unit but one that's in the process of dying."

4. We feel overwhelming guilt if we say NO.
Everywhere we turn we are faced with pleas for help. Our spouse, our boss, our children, our child's school, our elderly parents and friends cry out for our time and attention. Requests keep stacking up demanding something from us. It is too difficult to say NO, the guilt is too great.

5. We respond to the tyranny of the urgent.
Whenever there is a hint of a need, the hurried woman is on her feet to meet that need. The urgent can become tyrannical and make a slave of us so that we never accomplish those things which are important to us. We are too busy responding to the urgent.

6. We have such unrealistic expectations of ourselves.
We try so hard to be the perfect woman - friend, wife, mother, daughter and co-worker. We become so surprised at ourselves when we get sick or become tired of performing duty after duty.

7. We assume the responsibility is ours.
When there is a need, the hurried woman assumes she is to meet that need. She doesn't even give it a second thought…she plows right in, later wondering *why* she didn't think and pray first instead of assuming *SHE* was to do something.

Do you see yourself in any of the above reasons why you don't say NO?

How to Say No

"But above all, my brethren, do not swear, either by heaven or by earth or with any other oath. But let your yes be yes, and your no, no, lest you fall into judgment."
James 5:12.

Now that we see the dangers of not saying NO to some demands and the reasons why we don't say NO, we can certainly see why NO in our vocabulary is necessary. Now we can discuss HOW to say NO.

1. Listen to the totality of what is being asked before you respond.
The hurried woman jumps in and says YES before she even has all of the facts. For example, when asked to type a resume for a friend, does she also factor in the time for the cover letter, envelope, making copies. consultation and corrections? Only after she listens to the entire task asked

of her, should she prayerfully consider if this is something she should be doing.

2. Say NO after you have given yourself time to weigh the pros and cons.
Too often we hurried women think we need to respond immediately to a request. We don't take time to think a matter through from various viewpoints and to pray about what God wants. Instead we say yes and then go on to the next disaster. It would be far better to say, "Let me get back to you with my answer."

3. Say NO politely and firmly, don't waffle.
Can't we just hear ourselves as we waffle, "Well, let me see what will work out…I'm not sure…Aunt Maude may need me that day…I'd like to…but let me see what develops…."

We give false hope when we give the wishy washy answer of maybe yes or maybe no. It would be far kinder to come right out and say NO if that is what we intended and need to say.

4. Say NO without all of the reasons, excuses and rationalizations.
"It just won't work out" is a far better phrase than the 3000 words we use to cover the guilt we feel when we say NO.

5. As we say NO, we can kindly offer an alternative.
For example, "It just won't work out for me to sew 3000 buttons on the banner but I do know a lady who loves to sew on buttons…." You get the idea. Offering alternatives can soften a NO and provide a constructive alternative.

"But let your 'Yes' be 'Yes,' and your 'No,' 'No.'"
Matthew 5:37

Given this information, are there some tasks you need to say NO to in your life right now?

SIMPLIFY YOUR RELATIONSHIPS

– Balance Your and Your Children's Needs
– The Sandwich Generation
– Prioritize Your Friendships
– How to Be a Friend
– How to Keep a Friendship Growing
– Practical Tips to Stay Connected
– How to Renew a Lost Friendship
– Dating Thoughts
– Holidays
– Give Them and Yourself the Gift of Your Time

Baltasar Gracian, a Spanish Jesuit scholar wisely stated:

> "Look for friends who can last, and when they're new, be satisfied that one day they will be old. The best ones of all are those well salted, with whom we have shared bushels of experience. Life without friends is a wasteland."

Family and friends are treasures and are to be treated as such.

If we are married, our best friend should be our spouse. They deserve the highest priority, above children, friends and other family members as you become one.

"For this reason a man shall leave his father and mother and be joined to his wife, and the two shall become one flesh; so then they are no longer two, but one flesh. Therefore what God has joined together, let not man separate."
Mark 10:7-9

If we are blessed with children, some our most precious friends should be those little people. They have a priority because, without you, their basic needs won't be met and they won't grow into healthy, self-sufficient adults. Of course, we still maintain our spouse as our priority but our children must be honored with top ranking, too. It's as simple as that.

"Children are a gift from the Lord;
they are a reward from Him."
Psalm 127:3

Balancing Your and Your Children's Needs

In the process of keeping our children as a priority, it is important to keep in mind the balancing of parent's needs and children's needs.

First, it is SO important, if married, to keep your relationship with your spouse fresh. Date nights with just the two of you can lend itself to good conversation without the little people interrupting every two seconds.

Second, it is important to realize that good parenting is a balancing act. Ideally, the scales should remain balanced between parents' and children's needs. Tipped too far in one direction, the family becomes child-centered. That is never healthy for the children or the parents. Tipped too far the other direction, the parent or parents becomes me-centered. A balanced family-centered approach is the best of both worlds. Each family member's needs are to be met but not at the expense of other family members or of the family as a whole.

Third, it is important to realize that each daily decision we make affects the balance we are trying to attain and maintain in our families. Wisdom is needed for each decision.

Yes, good parenting is a balancing act! But we can do it, one decision at a time.

"Take heed that ye despise not one of these little ones; for I say unto you, That in heaven their angels do always behold the face of my Father which is in heaven."
Matthew 18:10-11

The Sandwich Generation

As we become older and see our children leave home, it may now be our turn to care for our own parents. Many books have been written on this subject so I won't go into detail here. Take some time, and research what will be needed, talk over with your parents what *they* envision for their future years. Sadly, funerals may need to be planned as well as the breaking up of their home and their belongings disbursed. What do they want done?

About 25 years ago, my parents asked if I would be the executrix of their estate. At the time, I lived 3000 miles away from them, was married and had two children; one of whom was a preschooler. I knew I could not do justice to what they wanted done so requested that my sibling take over those duties. Thankfully, that worked out for the best for my parents who subsequently needed serious medical attention, an assisted living move, and finally funeral details lovingly prepared.

Time management principles can be applied in that chapter of our lives, too, so we can love and serve our parents but not become burned out, neglecting ourselves or our own homes.

Also, don't forget to be a good friend to yourself! You are uniquely and wonderfully made. There will never be another *you.*

"You have searched me, Lord,
and You know me.
You know when I sit and when I rise;
You perceive my thoughts from afar.
You discern my going out and my lying down;
You are familiar with all my ways.
Before a word is on my tongue
You, Lord, know it completely."
Psalm 139:1-4

Please also remember that when we are told to love your neighbor as yourself, you must love *YOURSELF*, too.

Prioritize Your Friendships

In these times of social media where one can be in contact with 685 'friends', how can you simplify so that no one is neglected?

I believe the first order of business would be to prioritize the level of 'friendships'. Remember that some people are just acquaintances and not of the same status as a close friend whom you've enjoyed for 20 years.

Second, it is important to realize that relationships change over the years. If you are single, your 'friends' may be many and for a variety of reasons – jogging friends, work friends to mention just two.

If one becomes married, priorities change. A spouse deserves the highest priority over other friends. Plus, you would probably develop friendships with other couples along the way.

When children arrive, your sphere of friendships grow from play groups to school activities and so much more. It's an ever-changing life.

How to be a Friend

"As iron sharpens iron, so one person sharpens another."
Proverbs 27:17

To have a friend, first one must be a friend. The following are some of the qualities found between friends in a healthy, growing relationship:

* There is a willingness to nurture growth in each other.

* Each listens with her heart – not only to what is said but to what is not said.

* Trustworthiness is exhibited in matters discussed in confidence.

* Patience and forgiveness are practiced for inadequacies and mistakes.

* Through the inevitable joys and sorrows of life, being available to each other during those times is an essential ingredient.

* Relationships take time and effort. A marriage or family needs attention if it is to remain healthy.

* Extended family, too, must be taken into consideration.

* Healthy relationships take thought and care.

There is no way that we can give equal attention to 685 friends so we must prioritize, as much as possible, the people in our lives.

It is also important to remember that friendships should NOT be one sided unless it is directed by God and is a therapeutic relationship – built around one person helping another. If one person gives, gives, gives and all the other person does is take, that is a one sided relationship. Be careful! The life can be sucked right out of you if you are the person who continually gives unless that is what God directs you to do with that particular person. That includes a marriage relationship, too. A relationship means *TWO* people.

How to Keep a Friendship Growing

The following suggestions can help keep any friendship, old and new, growing:

1. Make time.
If we wait until we find the time to develop friendships, we will never do it. We must make the time. Specific time must be set aside for your relationship to grow and prosper.

2. Take the initiative.
Your friend is probably as busy as you are. Don't wait for her to take action. Taking the initiative shows you really care.

3. Keep in touch regularly.
In these days of texting, e-mail, social media and postage stamps or the phone, there is almost no excuse for neglecting to keep in touch on a regular basis.

Practical Tips to Stay Connected

Here are some ways to keep in touch and nurture your friendships whether you live near or far from your friend:
* Set date nights with your spouse.
* Spend time with your children one on one to make them feel special.
* Leave a humorous greeting on her voice mail.
* Text to reach out.
* Establish a tradition special to both of you.
* Send a card for no other reason than to show you were thinking of her.
* Include her in your daily walking and exercise regime.
* Find out the best calling plan if this is a long distance friend.
* Send photos.
* Save links and articles which you know would be of interest to her.
* Provide a home-cooked meal, delivered to her door during a time of illness or crisis.
* Set up a play date if you both have children. Let your children see what friends mean to each other.
* Go out for dessert, a Victorian tea or an ethnic meal.
* Swap recipes.
* Learn a new craft together. Take a basket weaving, quilting or painting class together just for fun.

Be creative in how you nurture your friendships. After all, treasures are to be enjoyed!

How to Renew a Lost Friendship

If you have a friend from the past with whom you haven't been in contact for years, chances are you may have to do a little detective work. Be creative – contact someone from your old neighborhood, ask a relative, ask a mutual friend or look on the Internet.

If your old friend also expresses an interest in re-connecting, proceed thoughtfully and with renewed care.

Dating Thoughts

If you are single, a word about dating would be wise to consider. Dating, as we know, can be much more complex now, especially with the online dating possibilities.

It is wise to follow the principles of building a friendship first whether dating begins online or through more traditional methods. It usually takes four seasons to really get to know a person. Marriage, which is supposed to be 'until death do us part', must be entered into cautiously! Knowing who that other person is in as many situations as possible, helps us to make a wise choice.

Ask yourself if that is someone with whom you want to link your life, your home, your finances, your children. What kind of a relationship do they have with their family? How do they treat their mother? What do their friends think of them? Are they courteous to those who serve them in restaurants? Are they courteous at *all* times to you? Are they willing to wait a year in order to get to know each other or do they want to jump into marriage right away? Are they isolating you from your family and friends? Are they jealous of how you spend your time and with whom?

All of these things, if red flags are seen, should be taken very seriously. You may need to slow down or STOP.

Some things to consider:
*You can only get to know someone really well if you observe them, listen to their words and watch their behavior. If their words don't match their behavior, they are not for you.

* If you think you can change them, think again…and again.

* Are you are being love bombed (defined as an attempt to influence a person by demonstrations of attention and affection). Love bombing can be used in different ways and can be used for either a positive or negative purpose.

*Give the hormones time to level off before you make any decision to become more serious than just friends.

Marriage is serious and, as we know, 'falling in love' often pushes aside common sense in our choice of a mate for life. It takes a great deal of time, effort and expense to untangle two lives physically, emotionally, financially and legally. Dating is serious and should not be entered into lightly! Nor should marriage.

"To acquire wisdom is to love oneself."
Proverbs 4:7

Holidays

Take a few minutes and think back to your childhood. Which holiday memories stand out as being extra special to you? Now think of the same holidays you celebrate today as an adult. How can you include some of those special traditions in the holidays that you celebrate now? What can you do to make your holidays less stressful and more meaningful?

The following are some time management tips to help you create an enjoyable season for yourself and for those whom you love – family and friends.

* Picture your ideal holiday season
Use your imagination to decide how you want your holiday season to unfold. Just remember that no season or certain day is totally perfect, so be realistic.

* Re-think outgrown holiday traditions
Take some time to think of the four or five most important attributes of the holidays which you would like to keep and embellish.

* Start a holiday planning notebook
Dividing it into sections or online, assemble a special *notebook* from which you can work. At the end of the holidays, record what went well and what you would change for the next year.

* Create a special holiday calendar
Place on the calendar all of those events which are most important to you during the season. When your calendar is

sufficiently filled, begin to say "NO" to all other invitations and possibilities.

* Plan to attend religious services
Take time to reflect on the meaning of the holiday you are celebrating. Decide which holiday services mean the most to you and attend those.

* Make a list of gift ideas
Be creative! A thoughtful gift doesn't have to be expensive. Homemade gifts are always appreciated. Jot down your ideas for each person in your notebook. As you find or create the treasures, cross them off your list. Don't forget to set aside a few last minute gifts for emergencies.

* Write a holiday card list
What a great opportunity the holidays are to communicate with friends. Make a master list for each year's use, updating as needed. Take advantage and send a note or letter with the card! Keep your list manageable so that it isn't a burden. Add a copy of a newsy letter with a personal note in each card. Begin early – right after Thanksgiving. Do a few every day and enjoy the process. Ordering stamps by mail can save precious time, too.

* Decorate simply
Decide which decorations you like best and eliminate the ones which are outdated, faded and have lost their appeal.

* Plan for overnight guests
Make a list of expected guests and then plan meals and activities allowing plenty of time to enjoy one another.

* Plan meals for the holidays
Perhaps you have always had the holiday family dinner at your house and have always cleaned and cooked the entire weekend beforehand. If you have found yourself frazzled and exhausted in the past, perhaps it is time to rethink the tradition. Here are some suggestions:

– Have a potluck with everyone bringing a dish.
– Opt to have a simple brunch, tea or dessert only.
– If anyone offers to help, take them up on it.

* Buying gifts
There is no need to go into debt for the holidays. Establish a budget and stick to it. Start holiday shopping early, following your list of gift ideas.
Other time-saving options include shopping by phone, or online. Gifts can even be shipped directly to the recipient.

* Wrapping gifts
Organize a special gift-wrapping center in your home. Wrap each gift as it is purchased or do it all at once. Have the following supplies on hand:

- Scissors
- Tape
- Ribbons and bows
- Gift Tags
- Wrapping paper

Time-saving options include letting a charitable organization wrap your gifts or asking the store to do it.

* Returning gifts
Keep away from waiting in long lines. If you have a gift to return, choose a time when the stores are least busy, well past the holidays. Free shipping and free return postage is great and is available for some items.

* Write thank you notes
As gifts are received and parties attended, promptly send thank you notes.

* Enlist help with holiday chores
Laundry will still need to be done as well as all other regular household duties. You can:
– Make a list of chores which need to be done.
– Ask for volunteers to help.
– Delegate chores if no volunteers step forward.
– Hire outside help for some of the heavier work.

Holidays are to be enjoyed. With well thought-out plans and good time management skills, you are on your way!

Give Them and Yourself the Gift of Your Time Year Round

When asked what they wanted for birthdays and holidays, 85% of those polled answered that they wanted more time with their family and friends. Why, then, do we allow so many other activities to intrude upon our time, to steal away the precious minutes and hours from doing what we really want to do?

We all know the importance of having FUN in our lives to maintain good mental health.

So many of us get on that merry-go-round and just don't give ourselves the gift of FUN and time.

What can be more precious than to just do something enjoyable and fun! Here are some suggestions:

* Research your family's roots
* Play volleyball year round
* Visit those who are lonely
* Make snow faces on trees to say "Welcome Home"
* Re-arrange a room
* Have popcorn in front of the fireplace
* Discuss the book you are reading
* Phone someone, just because
* Make snow creatures, snow chairs, tables and sofas
* Listen for winter bird sounds
* Gather winter wildflowers (they are already dried nicely)
* Learn to knit and make something special
* Plant herb seed inside to use for cooking
* Learn a foreign language together
* Bring miniature snowmen inside for a table centerpiece – place a pan under it to catch the melting snow
* Write a love poem
* Make paths in the snow, playing tag in the maze
* Share memories
* Do puzzles together
* Draw a seasonal scene
* Hike a nature center
* Learn to make a memory quilt
* Create a kitchen band to play along with music
* Sing together
* Plan your springtime garden, then plant, tend and harvest
* Create a family calendar for the year

* Visit the museum or a nature center
* Volunteer together
* Start a woodworking project
* Create an in-home library
* Assemble a special game and puzzle closet
* Start a collection – buttons, homeless dolls, teddy bears
* Explore a bird sanctuary
* Discover art at your local art center.
* Take a walk outside together on a starry night
* Give and receive a hug
* Share a kind, encouraging word
* Share laughter
* Listen with undivided attention
* Hold hands
* Watch television together
* Make eye contact
* Discuss the happenings of the day
* Ask questions of common interest
* Read together
* Bake some bread
* Visit other loved ones
* Have a thankful heart
* Clear out clutter together
* Write a letter to someone you love
* Play dress-up
* Ice skate
* Cook together
* Be cheerful
* Invite friends over
* Eat together at the dinner table every night
* Love a pet
* Exercise together
* Create a family recipe book

* Finish your children's baby books
* Learn to track animals in the snow
* Update the family photo album
* Establish a board game night
* Write your life story
* Finish up a craft project together

Yes, brightly wrapped presents may be a part of our birthday, special occasion or holiday celebrations. This year, however, let's make a point of giving the gift of ourselves and our time to loved ones. Isn't that what we all really want anyway?

In the process, you will probably find that YOU had a tremendous amount of fun.

SIMPLIFY YOUR POSSESSIONS

– Clutter Detector Test
– Clutter Causes Problems
– Clutter Causes More Problems
– Four Clutter Collector Types
– How to Set Ourselves Free From Clutter
– Proper Paper Processing

"Then He said to them, Watch out! Be on your guard against all kinds of greed; life does not consist in an abundance of possessions."
Luke 12:15

Now that you are learning to simplify your activities and relationships, you can turn your attention to simplifying your possessions. - by saying NO to clutter.

Clutter causes stress! We have a deep-seated anxiety that *something* could happen to our *stuff.*

We pay good money to accumulate more and care for it, causing financial stress. Selfishness is reflected in the cry of the child in us as we scream, "I want it!". Divorce is often the result of financial woes. Embezzlement, theft and murder often reflect society's desire for more. And the ultimate cry of "I want it" is war.

Do you have a problem with clutter? Of wanting more? Do you experience stress in your life because of clutter?

Take the **CLUTTER DETECTOR TEST** and find out how you are doing in this area of your life.

1. I save junk mail for weeks and months. Some of it has never been opened.

2. I have missed paying a bill because I've misplaced it.

3. I've missed an event because I've misplaced the invitation.

4. I miss out on phone messages because they get lost in my phone or I don't have paper and pen to take down the information.

5. My bulletin board has layers of out-of-date material on it.

6. I can file something on Monday and can't find it by Friday.

7. My desk is full of layers and layers of miscellaneous papers and dust.

8. I keep a calendar (paper or online) but never keep it up to date with commitments on it.

9. I have so many books that I must store some in boxes in the attic, basement and/or garage. My e-reader is so full, I don't know what I have there.

10. Many of the stored names and other pertinent information I need are out of date.

11. I save boxes and envelopes of all sizes.

12. I save ideas on scraps of paper which have never been filed so I can't find them to act upon.

13. I keep ball point pens that skip and felt tip markers that are dry.

14. I have cookbooks and recipes that I never use.

15. I have stored extra pounds on my body.

16. I save bottles, plastic bags, twist ties and plastic containers so my cupboards are a jumbled mess.

17. I clip coupons I'll never use and keep expired coupons for months without noticing.

18. I have kitchen appliances and gizmos that I never use.

19. I save paper and plastic bags of all sizes and shapes.

20. My pots, pans and lids are so disorganized that I hate to cook.

21. I have so many plastic containers full of leftovers that I never know what is in them or when the leftovers should be thrown out.

22. I own more than two sets of dishes.

23. I have too many kitchen towels and aprons.

24. If I need a screwdriver or hammer, it takes me more than 60 seconds to find it.

25. I have half finished projects all over the house.

26. I have outdated patterns and fabric stashed around the house, garage, attic and basement.

27. I have do-it-yourself books and pieces of lumber stored in the basement, garage or storage shed.

28. My photos need to be dated and put in albums.

29. I have sports equipment in closets, in the basement and attic and rarely use it.

30. I have boxes of heirlooms from my parents and their parents.

31. I save batteries which are almost dead or ARE dead.

32. I have a closet full of clothes but often have trouble figuring out what to wear.

33. I have various sizes of clothing…just in case.

34. I own shoes that hurt my feet and which I never wear.

35. I save old eyeglasses, watches and clocks which don't work.

36. My purse/briefcase contains and weighs too much.

37. I have jewelry I never wear.

38. I save old cologne or perfume even though I hate the odor.

39. My furniture lines every wall and I often bump into it.

40. I keep things that need to be repaired, mended or cleaned and never get around to it.

41. My garage is so full that I can't get my car inside.

42. I have old gum wrappers, receipts and fast food garbage on the seats and floor of my car.

43. I have medicine cabinet contents which contain outdated items.

44. My attic and basement are full of boxes of family mementos and I don't remember what is there.

45. I routinely lose or misplace things.

46. I save things given to me as gifts even though I never use them and don't even like them.

47. I have to rent extra storage space because I have so many possessions.

48. I sometimes feel overwhelmed by the clutter of my possessions.

49. I watch junk TV shows.

50. My vacuum cleaner has attachments which I've never used and don't know what they are.

51. I brought disposable things home from the hospital after being ill but never use them.

52. I buy souvenirs on my vacations and then wonder where to put them.

53. My pet has his own toys, grooming and kitchen clutter.

54. I save used wrapping paper and old birthday cards.

55. I have old and outdated maternity clothes stored away.

56. I save children's outgrown toys, school papers and clothing.

57. I wish I could simplify my life!

Clutter Causes Problems

We must remember, however, that if an item builds, edifies and enriches us, it isn't clutter. For example, I paid a visit to my parents' home. Each morning as I awoke on a makeshift bed on the floor in the living room, I would see shelves with books and knick knacks. One item puzzled me – it looked like an ugly mug, completely out of place in my parent's classy looking living room. Finally, on my last day there, I looked at it more closely – it was a mug commemorating a 50 year high school reunion - not a piece of clutter to my parents, but a precious memento of enjoyable days long ago.

What's the big deal about clutter? Let me quote from Don Aslett's book, *Clutter's Last Stand*:

> "Clutter stifles and robs us of freedom because it requires so much of our time to tend. We have no time to have fun, to do the things we really want to do. Not only are our houses, drawers, closets and vehicles so crowded we can't breathe, but our minds, emotions and relationships, too, are crowded into dullness and immobility. We're so surrounded with stuff, we don't even have time for the people who mean the most to us."

From this quote, you can see that it may not be the clutter itself that we need to be concerned about but what clutter does to us!

Below are a few rhetorical questions to think about:

1. Have you replaced thinking, living and loving with the pursuit of and care of things?

2. Has the quality of your life become watered down as you fritter away time and money on the accumulation of things and their care?

3. Are you free for action or are you bogged down in clutter?

4. Are you ready to taste the new and fresh or are you gripped in the clutter of the past such as bitterness and blame?

5. Are some of your routines just clutter?

6. Have you insulated yourself in clutter so that you don't allow others to get close to you?

Clutter Causes MORE Problems

1. Storing clutter costs $.10 to $10.00 per square foot according to Stephanie Culp in *How to Conquer Clutter.* The more we fill our homes with clutter, the larger the area we think we need. Thus, we end up paying hard-earned money to collect and store our *stuff.* We are no longer satisfied with stashing things in basements and attics, now we build four car garages, storage sheds and rent storage places away from home.

How much are YOU spending to store your 'stuff'?

2. Clutter deteriorates.
Too often we put our extra 'stuff' in the attic, basement and garage only to find it ruined by mildew, heat or water from a leak.

Are you storing extra 'stuff' safely where it won't be harmed?

3. Clutter clutters.
Most of our housework is shifting 'stuff' from place to place before we even start dusting and sweeping. If we ever have to move, it is more expensive financially and more difficult logistically because of our 'stuff'.

How long would it take you to dust and vacuum if all the clutter is gone?

4. Clutter controls.
We are so busy keeping our clutter under control, we have no time left for the new and fresh things that could come our way. We are being controlled by 'stuff'.

Is your clutter controlling YOU?

5. Clutter creates an image.
If we live in a cluttered mess, people could wonder about our organizational skills in other areas, too.

When someone first walks into your home, what do they see? Orderliness or chaos?

Four Clutter Collector Types

How, then, can we set ourselves free from clutter? As you survey your own situation, you will find there will be four kinds of people:

Type A is the kind of person who hates clutter of any kind and keeps a pair of tweezers at hand to constantly pull the least bit out.

Type B is the kind of person who finds that clutter is a nuisance. It aggravates her but clutter does not impair her life since she periodically deals with it.

Type C is the kind of person who LOVES clutter surrounding her in every nook and cranny. Clutter seems not to be a problem at all even though there is TONS of it.

Type D is the kind of person whose home and office are considered a red alert area – there are stacks everywhere and there could be an avalanche at any moment.

What type are you?

How to Set Ourselves Free From Clutter

Some experts in clutter recommend that the solution to the clutter problem is better storage. They advise adding more shelves, baskets, bins, blanket storage boxes, can racks, car organizers, crates, foot lockers, gift wrap organizers, hat boxes, lid storage racks, lingerie boxes, mug racks, shoe bags, shoe racks, shoe stackers and so on. Do we really need $100 drawer organizers to organize our earrings? Don Aslett, author of *Clutter's Last Stand,* calls these junk bunkers - the seven story tool boxes, the four story sewing boxes and the extra room added on to store more stuff.

Aren't we just organizing and re-organizing our clutter so that we can keep it? Isn't the real problem that of *owning too much*?

I love this quote, again by Aslett: "Cleaning and organizing a house is one of life's best seminars in self-improvement." I often tell myself that and begin feeling quite pleased with myself.

The 80/20 Rule - The Pareto Principle

Let's deal with this *too much* issue. Have you heard of the 80/20 Rule? Eighty percent of value will come from twenty percent of the items we own. Therefore, 80% of our *things* aren't really necessary. We use them infrequently or not at all. We use only 20% of our cosmetics, find value in only 20% of our mail and wear only 20% of our clothing as stated by Susan Stautberg and Marcia Worthing in *Balancing Acts.*

The Amish people are a good example of living simply. Most of us wouldn't want to use horse and buggy again, but we could strive for their example in living simply.

I always smile as I think - why not put all of our belongings on digital images? Then we wouldn't have to keep the stuff, clean it, move it and polish it. We could just carry the pictures of our stuff and look at them when we want to. How convenient is that!

In a book, *Material World* by Peter Menzel, 16 photographers journeyed to 30 countries to live with 30 families for a week. At the end of the week, each family placed all of their belongings in front of their homes for a family photo. What an interesting, powerful and educational view of how others live. We would clearly see how much we own in comparison to the rest of the families of the world!

How long would it take you to move all of your belongings in front of your home? An hour, a week, a month?

Ready for Action … Eliminate Excess

Once you have surveyed your surroundings and have decided that a change in the amount of clutter is needed, you will need to quit making excuses. Yes, you may use it or repair it or give it away to someone special…later. Yet who has more time later?

Even if you plan to do something about your clutter when you retire, have you noticed lately how busy retired people are? If you don't take care of clutter now, you won't later…for the same reasons.

When you decide to do something about your clutter, it is important to *define for yourself* which clutter needs to be dealt with. Each woman must establish for herself the level of order and cleanliness she wants to maintain for herself and for her family.

When you are ready to take action, it is of utmost importance not to become a decluttering fanatic so that you drive everyone around you crazy with your decluttering frenzy. Keep a sane, balanced approach! (See the end of this chapter for a fun decluttering schedule)!

Always do your regular housework, meal preparation and laundry first so that you can stay on your regular household schedule as you declutter. Work for short periods of time each day so that you don't create havoc all through the day in every room of the house. Do a closet or drawer; don't try to tackle an entire house in one day.

You may, however, decide to do a marathon decluttering job by setting aside a week or a month to get it ALL done. In that case, continue to plan our your strategy so that all of your surroundings are not in chaos and you are able to keep up with daily chores.

How do *you* want to declutter – bit by bit or by holding a marathon?

Take some time and go room by room. In each room visualize your ideal for that particular room.

Now establish specific goals for each room.

Decide if more storage containers or shelves are needed to better organize what you do keep. Be careful, however, not to purchase more storage aids which will just add more clutter to your life.

Categorize Your Possessions

How do you decide which is *good stuff* and which is clutter?

As you look at each item in your drawer or closet, decide in which category it falls:

Category A – Used frequently and can't live without.
Keept these items within easy to reach places usually between eye and hip level. An example is a paring knife which you probably use many times a day.

Category B – Used occasionally and would enjoy keeping.
These items can be stored up high or down low or behind your A items. An example would be the Thanksgiving platter you only use once a year.

Category C – Of sentimental value to keep or store.
These items can be stored out of sight in a safe place. Maybe eventually you will want to part with some of them, too. An example would be baby clothes from your last child.

Category D – Used infrequently or not at all – you can live without these items.
Be brave on this one. Get rid of these items!

Category E – Must be filed for future use.
This includes all important papers. A filing system must be established for these items (more about paper processing later).

Have Everything in its Proper Place

As you begin to find places for your A and B items, keep in mind an important principle: *Have a place for everything and have everything in its place.* The place where you decide to keep an item should be in a logical, convenient location where all family members know where that object belongs.

For example, if the kitchen scissors are best kept in a kitchen drawer, then that's where they belong when they're not being used. Everyone knows where the scissors are when they want to use them and everyone knows where the scissors belong when they are finished using them.

The In and Out Rule

Simply stated, the In and Out Rule means that if you bring something *new* into your home, get rid of something *old.* I have been attempting to live by that rule and it really works!

If you find yourself living in a pack rat's den and know that you don't have the energy or stamina to deal with it, professionals are available to help in a compassionate manner.

The Six Bag Technique

Using either paper bags, plastic grocery bags or large plastic bags (depending on how bad the problem is), get ready to declutter extensively.

The following are some possibilities for disposing of your *stuff*.

Garbage

Why are we so afraid of throwing things away? Why do we keep file after file and never tried recipes or crafts we've never attempted? Why do we keep broken wagons and bikes? Our closets are stuffed with worn out clothing we will never wear. The list goes on and on. Be brave, throw away bad junk!

Give to Family and Friends

Be careful here. You don't want to lose your friends and be cast out of your family because you passed *your* junk to *them*. Give only good stuff.

Give to Charitable Causes

The Gospel Mission, Salvation Army and church sales are great places to donate usable but unwanted items. A coat which is not needed by you may be much needed by someone else.

Recycle

Recycling is big right now. Take advantage of the recycling center and curbside pick-up to keep house and yard clutter under control. Consignment resale shops are excellent places, too. Check out what is available in your area. Yard and garage sales are a great deal of work but fun, too. One year when my family and I were moving out of the area, we held a yard sale. All of a sudden I was meeting neighbors I never knew I had. I decided that the next time I move, I will have a yard sale in my *new* neighborhood.

Storage
Be careful! Space costs money, remember?

Put Aside to Sort in One Month, One Year
Perhaps you just can't part with those old baby clothes but in five years you may be able to do so.

Proper Paper Processing

How much time do we waste shuffling needless papers back and forth each day? We know we need to do something before the avalanche of warranties, daily mail, guarantees, recipes, bills, receipts, invitations, announcements, books, magazines, photos and phone messages smother us once and for all. What can we do about this profusion of paper?

Let's re-think the entire scenario. Why not set up and run your home as if you were CEO of a mini-corporation? Look around to see where you can create a special place to process papers. The place you choose, whether an ornate oak desk in your own home office or a small fabric covered table in the corner of the kitchen, should be dedicated to just that job - processing papers which enter your life on a daily basis.

Once you have established a place to work, you need a system for handling the paper processing. Basically, there are six choices for handling each piece of paper that comes your way:

Recycle it
We are fortunate in some communities to have places or bins provided to recycle. We can even create a compost pit in the back yard to recycle.

Throw it Away

Be generous with this action! Place a large wastebasket near your *desk*. As you handle each piece of paper, ask yourself the following questions:

* Can I find this information elsewhere, as on the Internet?
* Will I ever use this information again?
* If I save this information, will it be outdated next week?
* Do I need this information for tax, legal, medical or personal reasons?
* Where am I going to keep this information to save it?

Pay It

* Establish a bill paying system that allows you to pay as many bills as possible at one sitting.
* Pay as many bills as possible the easy way – online or by auto deduct.
* Keep clear records and file copies of any financial transactions.
* Use a debit card or credit card when possible.

Do It

* Create a Master To Do List by writing down everything you can think of which must be done.
* Make a Daily To Do List, choosing three to five of the most important items at the top on your To Do List.
* Design a personal planner either online or on paper to track your To Do Lists, projects, mileage, expenses or any other pertinent information.
* Create a personal calendar which will keep dates and deadlines in front of you.
* Place a family calendar where everyone can see it. Use a different color marker for each family member.

* Post chore charts so everyone knows what is expected of him or her.
* Assemble and make copies of a Master Grocery List based on the layout of your grocery store.

Respond

* Create a Telephone Message Center. Even though you may have all of the information stored in your phone, continue to use an alphabetical card filing system.
* Establish a system to keep track of personal correspondence, when received and when answered.
* Fill out forms as quickly as possible, make a copy, file yours and return the other copy promptly.
* Shower invitations, wedding and graduation announcements usually require a response on your part. Enter the event on your calendar, assembling cards and gifts as needed.

Read It

Most of us are swamped with too much reading material. We may need to choose that which has the most meaning to us and let the rest go.

* Neatly stack reading material for those snatches of time when you can attack the stack.
* Cancel subscriptions that aren't a high priority.
* Cancel links which show up in your email inbox that you no longer want.
* Create a family library. Then set aside a bookcase for your personal books.
* Keep library books in a separate place so they don't become mixed in with your personal collection.
* Recycle. Newspapers can be sent to the recycling center.

Magazines can be donated to the library, family or friends. Read them and keep them moving.

File It

Whoever heard of running a corporation without a filing cabinet? Homes are like mini-corporations with the same need for organization. What should you put in your filing cabinet? File folders would be important, also!

* Family records such as birth certificates, social security cards, genealogical information, armed service data, diplomas and transcripts.
* Warranties, guarantees and instruction manuals plus a history of repairs – vehicle, appliances, roof, water heater.
* Medical and dental records, reports, prescriptions, vaccination dates, list of allergies.
* New, untried recipes.
* Project directions, sources for craft materials, patterns… the list is endless….
* Keep your family photos labeled and safely displayed or stored.
* Use a box to store your child's drawings, poems and creations. Yearly, create a notebook or scrapbook representing the best of that year. Be brave, throw the rest away when appropriate.

Practice proper paper processing. It's a real time saver!

Just for Fun

Take one activity per day and declutter bit by bit for a month. See how good you will feel about yourself!

1. Clean out your purse

2. Clean out the inside of your vehicle
3. Purge your closet of too large, too small and out of style clothing
4. Sort shoes – those which are out of fashion, too small, too large and those which hurt your feet
5. Clean out one drawer at a time
6. Sort and re-arrange your crafts – paper, yarn, fabric, scrapbooking
7. Sort and re-range DVDs, videos, CDs and any other entertainment items
8. Take care of that pile of papers (see Proper Paper Processing)
9. Update your medicine cabinet contents
10. Clean off any surface area – tables, cabinets, counters, beds
11. Sort and clean out two kitchen cabinets at a time
12. Go through your kitchen utensil drawer and purge doubles
13. Donate old books you no longer want
14. Update your wallet contents
15. Clean out your make-up drawer
16. Re-arrange your underwear and sock drawers
17. Organize your sheets, towels and other linen closet contents
18. Get rid of old and almost empty bathroom containers
19. Clean and re-arrange cleaning supplies
20. Sort through and get rid of old accessories – purses, hats, scarves and jewelry
21. Re-arrange refrigerator contents and throw away old leftovers or items
22. Pass along your children's old toys, organize what remains
23. Re-rrange the basement and get rid of excess

24. Donate old games, organize what remains
25. Clean out the freezer
26. Clean out and organize under the kitchen sink
27. Organize your pots and pans
28. Organize your recipes
29. Re-arrange baking and serving bowls
30. Declutter food storage containers
31. Now you are FREE to ENJOY!!!

CHAPTER 3

SPECIALIZE - NOW SAY YES!

"But He said to me, 'My grace is sufficient for you, for My power is made perfect in weakness.' Therefore I will boast all the more gladly about my weaknesses, so that Christ's power may rest on me."
II Corinthians 12:9

– Visualize Your Ideal Life
– Set Goals to Get There
– Establish Priorities
– Specialize by Personality Type
– Specialize by Season of Life
– Something to Think About
– If Change is Needed
– Caution

We've talked about stepping off the merry-go- round to gain perspective, to evaluate ourselves and to see where we are headed. We've also talked about simplifying – saying NO to a clutter of activities, relationships and possessions.

Now that our calendar and homes are being simplified, we can gain the ability to specialize in those activities which we want to do in our lives. We can begin to say YES!

Many professions encourage specialization. Doctors, lawyers, nurses and teachers specialize. We, as women, need to specialize so that what we do will be done well and be carried out with enjoyment!

For example: If one is getting married or is married already, wouldn't it be wise to read all you can about what it is to be a wife? Or if you were going to have a baby, to read all you can about the development of your child? YES! We, as women, must be educated in regard to the roles we play throughout the seasons of our lives! Most important, though, is to prayerfully listen to find out what God wants your life to look like.

Now let's look at your monthly schedule.

Look at your calendar for this month. Think about the number of items on it that you are doing just because it is expected of you but that you don't really *want* to do.

Look again at your calendar. Think about the number of items that you are doing because you *want* to and *choose* to do them.

Do you see an imbalance between *have to* and *want to*?

What we do with our time shouts loudly about what we value in our lives. For example, if we say we value our family above all else and then spend all of our time and energy on other things, we know we are lying to ourselves.

If we are to be effective in our homes, in the workplace and in our community, it is important to gain and maintain control of our lives so that the time we utilize will be used to accomplish what WE value in life.

Visualize Your Ideal Life

An ideal life is a hope, dream or picture of what you would like it to be. For example, you may want to be a better employee or you may want to be more active in your community or place of worship.

Take time to prayerfully picture yourself and what you would like your ideal life to look like.

As you think about your ideals, a picture of your hopes and dreams for yourself will emerge. You probably used the word *to be* or *to become.* In order to become something, you must *do* something. That's when goal setting enters the picture.

Set Goals to Get There

Whereas an ideal is a generalized picture in one's mind of what you want, the following pertains to goal setting and how you get to your ideals:

A Goal Is Specific.
A goal is something you can do to attain your ideal.

A Goal is Measurable.
You will know if you did it, didn't do it or only did it partially.

A Goal is Accomplishable.
A goal is *not* a pie in the sky idea but a task which you can do.

For example, if your ideal is to be a better employee, your goals (specific, measurable and accomplishable) may be the following:

1. To attend the seminar in the spring which will help update your skills.
2. To take allowed lunch times and breaks each day so that you can work more efficiently in the afternoon.
3. To have Friday reports completed by Thursday afternoon before you leave work.

For each ideal, take time to think about and list some goals you can set for yourself at home and at work.

Establish Priorities

Now what? Now you put first things first. You list your goals in order of importance – that's called establishing priorities. Some goals you may be able to do now and others may need to wait until you get the first goals achieved successfully. You want to reach your ideal life eventually, not burn out because you tried to do it all at once. Thus, put first things first.

Another concept to keep in mind as you are prioritizing your goals is to differentiate between people priorities and activity priorities. For example, it is more important to take your feverish daughter to the doctor (people priority) than it is to wash the kitchen floor (activity priority).

Take a look at your list of goals and number them in order of importance. Take your time.

In *Strategy for Living*, Dayton and Engstrom state:

> "Goals for which you have no priorities are useless. They will always be getting in the way of one another."

After setting your priorities for the day, week, month and/or year, if you do only one or two items listed, you know that you have accomplished the most important and the remainder of the list will be there for another day.

Specialize by Your Personality Type

If a person knows her personality type, life can become so much more enjoyable. If you know your type or bent, you can work *with* it and not fight against it. God created you exactly as you are and you need to value the person He wants you to be. Yes, we each can improve, keep our personality type under control, grow and change, but it is all-important to recognize who you are.

For example, I am a Type A Personality Type. That's how God wired me. There are strengths to every type. I must recognize and use those strengths but I also know that my personality type means I will probably always have a problem with trying to do too much, too fast. That tendency must be controlled or I suffer from it as do those around me.

If you've never taken a Personality Type Assessment, it might be fun for you to discover more of who you are. I found that the Myers-Briggs Personality Type Indicator can be a great help. Then you can extend your knowledge, recognizing your family and friends' *bent* and that will help you to be more in tune with others.

Here is an example of what you will find with the Myers-Briggs test:

At the heart of Myers-Briggs theory are four preferences. Do you prefer to deal with:

- People and things or ideas and information
- Facts and reality or possibilities and potential
- Logic and truth or values and relationship
- A lifestyle that is well-structured or one that goes with the flow

In the Myers- Briggs theory, for each pair you will usually exhibit one style over the other.

Extroversion and Introversion - The first pair of styles is concerned with the direction of your energy. If you prefer to direct your energy to deal with people, things, situations, or the outer world, then extroversion is your preference. If you prefer to direct your energy to deal with ideas, information, explanations or beliefs, or the inner world, then your preference is for Introversion.

Sensing and Intuition - The second pair concerns the type of information/things that you process. If you prefer to deal with facts, what you know, to have clarity, or to describe what you see, then your preference is for Sensing. If you prefer to deal with ideas, look into the unknown, to generate new possibilities or to anticipate what isn't obvious, then your preference is for Intuition.

Thinking and Feeling – The third pair reflects your style of decision-making. If you prefer to decide on the basis of objective logic, using an analytical and detached approach, then your preference is for Thinking. If you prefer to decide using values – i.e. on the basis of what or who you believe is important – then your preference is for Feeling.

Judgment and Perception – The final pair describes the type of lifestyle you adopt. If you prefer your life to be planned, stable and organized, then your preference is for Judging (not to be confused with 'judgmental', which is quite different). If you prefer to go with the flow, to maintain flexibility and respond to things as they arise, then your preference is for Perception.

The theory was developed by Katharine Briggs and Isabel Briggs-Myers. To learn more and discover your preferences, complete their free online personality questionnaire. It provides online reports that give you a deeper understanding. They will also help you to choose a career, deepen your self-awareness, develop your leadership potential and improve relationships.

Specialize by Season of Life

Women's lives are made up of a sequence of seasons. The following is a brief overview of the progression of seasons in our lives, some of which may overlap:

Unmarried young woman
Unmarried student
Unmarried with a career
Married with a career
Adult with young children
Adult with school age children
Adult with teenagers

Adult with grown children

Adult who has returned to work with children

Adult with aging parents

Adult who is retired

Most of us try to do it all at once. We are married, have a career, are raising young children and we try to go to school full time. We have approximately 75-90 years to do it all…so why do we try to do it all at once…and now?

"There is a time for everything,
and a season for every activity under the heavens:

a time to be born and a time to die,
a time to plant and a time to uproot,
a time to kill and a time to heal,
a time to tear down and a time to build,
a time to weep and a time to laugh,
a time to mourn and a time to dance,

a time to scatter stones and a time to gather them,
a time to embrace and a time to refrain from embracing,
a time to search and a time to give up,
a time to keep and a time to throw away,

a time to tear and a time to mend,
a time to be silent and a time to speak,
a time to love and a time to hate,
a time for war and a time for peace."

Ecclesiastes 3:1-8

Are you living one season at a time or are you trying to live two or three seasons at the same time?

What season are you in right now?

Looking at our lives as a progression of seasons is healthy. Then we can *specialize* in certain areas during the different seasons.

Specializing in Your Work

"Whatever you do, work at it with all your heart, as working for the Lord, not for human masters."
Colossians 3:23

All we do should be done to the best of our abilities -- efficiently and thoroughly. We practice, make things more efficient, learn new ways and get more and more proficient in what we do whether at work or at home.

For example, most of us women have done laundry since we were in our teens. Have we perfected this bit of work we do? Are we as efficient and effective as possible? Let's look at laundry as an example of specializing in our work at home.

Laundry 101

If you listen carefully, you may hear the flapping of freshly laundered clothes on the clothesline or tumbling softly in the dryer.

Whether you are a CEO, teacher, factory worker, nurse, parent or administrative assistant, we usually find ourselves in the laundry room or laundromat at least once a week – usually more often.

Although many of us are experts in diverse areas, for some of us, the laundry process continually gets stalled. However, I think we will all agree that the laundry isn't really *done* until the clothes, bedding and towels are laundered, mended and ironed, then hung in an orderly fashion in the proper closet or folded neatly and placed in a drawer or on a shelf. The orderly flow of doing the laundry from beginning to end reflects good time management skills.

We have been doing laundry for thousands of years. Sure, we may have taken some hints from our grandmothers or mothers, but fabrics are different nowadays and the rushed pace of our lives is somehow quite different, too.

The following are some laundry tips which may be of help:

1. Stain Removal

There are miraculous products on the market today which make the stain removal process painless and quick. Make life easier on yourself – use them as soon as a stain appears, don't delay.

2. Sorting Laundry

Give each person in your household two laundry baskets and a laundry bag. As clothes are taken off, have them place white and light colored items in one basket, dark items in the second basket and delicate items in the bag. No more sorting is needed than that.

3. Laundering

It is important with our busy lives to establish a laundry schedule and stick to it as much as possible. We do have options. Here are a few:

* Have your children help. Children as young as eight, under your supervision, can be taught the entire laundry process and could be responsible for their own laundry.
* Hire the laundry done. Many laundromats have a four-minute laundry service - it takes two minutes to drop the laundry off, two minutes to pick it up and they do all the work.
* Change clothes less frequently.

4. Drying

If you dry your laundry on a clothesline, enjoy the out-of-doors, don't rush it! If children are nearby, have them hand the clothespins to you – involve them in the process. If you dry by machine, take the laundry out as soon as the cycle is finished to prevent wrinkling which necessitates more work.

5. Folding Laundry

Children as young as two can learn to match socks and fold simple items. Children love to help, let's allow them the opportunity to learn practical life skills.

6. Mending

* Gather your mending supplies and create an old fashioned mending basket. Mend while watching television in the evenings. You will be surprised how fast the pile shrinks.

* Keep your sewing machine ready. Make it your goal to weekly tend to any items which are missing buttons, have tears or hems which are falling.
* Hire mending, hemming and sewing done. There are businesses which specialize in this work or perhaps one of your children enjoys hand sewing.

7. Ironing
* Set up an Ironing Center with all needed items.
* Make the process enjoyable – play some music, listen to a book on tape or have a conversation with a child or your spouse.
* Establish one day per week to iron. Then do it all! This is a wiser use of time than getting the ironing board out and the iron hot every time an item is needed.
* Teach your children, male and female, to iron properly.
* Hire the ironing done - your local laundromat or dry cleaner would like your business.

8. Putting It Away
Family members know where and how they like their clothes kept. Try this: Assign each family member a laundry basket for clean clothes. As clothing is laundered and folded, the items can be placed in that person's basket. Give them the responsibility of putting their items away where and how they like.

9. Dry Cleaning
Choose one day per week or per month to drop off your dry cleaning. Do the same for picking it up. Do not make a special trip for this task but incorporate it in your round of other errands. Or purchase a dry cleaning kit (available at your local shopping center) which can be used at your

convenience in your dryer at home. Experts agree, however, that this method of dry cleaning is best used if clothing is only lightly soiled.

May we not only have freshly laundered clothing, all neatly put away, but may we hum a tune as the machines help us in our duties. May we also do a little hop, skip and dance around the clothesline as we enjoy the bright, sunny days ahcad. Let's enjoy life!

Meal Preparation 101

Another area which can be made more efficient is that of meal preparations which involves not only having the skills to actually cook the meal but to learn good meal planning which includes the nutritional aspects, cost and specific likes and dislikes. A recipe may be needed as a reminder of necessary ingredients while shopping. I personally have created a master grocery list from which I pull items needed for that week, so I don't forget the basic needs of the pantry and household.

I can still remember my grandmother, 60 years ago, sitting in her big overstuffed easy chair, calling 'Brownie' at the market where she bought food. She would read off her grocery shopping list to him and he would deliver to her door. She is probably smiling down as she sees how things work today; we go to our computer or apps to order groceries and they are delivered to our door!

Even after the meal has been prepared and eaten, there is still time management involved in clean up, putting away the leftovers, running the dishwasher and training the children in basic life skills.

Think about what other areas of your life which could be streamlined so that you can use your time more wisely. Maybe having some time even for some fun things.

Something to Think About

Please be aware that women are very creative and flexible in their job choices – some work part-time, some work out of their own homes, some do time sharing and some are self-employed. According to surveys presently conducted, over 70 percent of women in the United States work outside of the home. Remember, however, not all of those surveyed work 40 hours a week outside the home. The 70 percent makes it look like *everyone is doing it* and we try to *do it all* right along with *everybody else.*

Here are a few questions to ask yourself if you are working in the home, at a home-based business or outside the home:

* Does your working inside or outside of the home push you into a higher tax bracket?

* What is your gross income?

* How much does it *cost* you to work outside of the home in regard to:
  Taxes
  Social security
  Childcare
  Food and beverage items (lunch, snacks, water)
  Transportation (vehicle, gas, insurance, upkeep)
  Household help (jobs hired out)

Wardrobe (clothing and shoes needed)
Conveniences (such as eating out)
Other

* How many hours do you work?

* Divide your net yearly income by hours worked.

* Is your time worth *more* than that or are you satisfied with your earnings?

If Change is Needed

If you do find yourself overloaded and decide to go from full time to part time work or even to remain home full time, some plans need to be established. You will especially need to talk this over with your family. The following may be of help in your decisions:

1. Determine a possible target date for the change. Don't give notice at your place of employment yet, do some evaluating first.

2. Try to live for a few months on the income that you will have after you change your working conditions. Creatively consider how you can stretch the dollars you will have.

3. Set aside the money you earn during that time as a cushion for later, if needed.

4. Establish a weekly routine for your new schedule. Quitting work and landing yourself at home full time can be a shock for anyone. Plan ahead. Make a list of all of those jobs and fun things you've been wanting to do but never had the time.

Recently more women are leaving the workplace realizing that they want something more for themselves and their families than a paycheck and the hurried woman lifestyle. They are beginning to *specialize* in the activities which result in attaining their ideals.

The purpose of this book is not to encourage you to stay home full time or to work outside the home full time or part time. Each lifestyle may be necessary during different seasons in our lives. The purpose here is to help you look at what *you* want in your life presently and to help you strive for that

Caution

A caution is needed here. Even if a woman is at home full time, she can still be absent from her family as her time is gobbled up by her cell phone, TV, committee meetings and the variety of other activities which steal away her time from the things that matter the most.

Pearl S. Buck gives such a caution in her book *To My Daughters, With Love* which was published in 1967 and is still true today:

> "It takes real self discipline to be a good housewife and not all housewives are

> homemakers. Some women put house ahead of home and then they are only cleaning women and cooks. Some women are lazy and cannot discipline themselves to do each day's work well enough to create a place of beauty and order for her family life. It is very easy, when husband has gone to work and children to school, to settle down with another cup of coffee and the radio, television or even the telephone. The undisciplined woman in the home can cheat on the job, too, if she has no conscience. Home can be a place of escape from reality if a woman lets herself begin to slide. Women are as human as men and some people work only when they are watched. I suppose that such women had better go out to work where they can be watched and bring back money, at least."

Those are strong words!

If you have decided to be home full-time for any reason, perhaps raising young children or caring for elderly parents, you can take classes, read books, learn new skills, do volunteer work or find new recreational activities. The list is endless. Take advantage of the time for personal development. If and when you do return to the workplace, you will be *more* than prepared for a new season of your life.

"Whatever you do, work at it with all your heart, as working for the Lord, not for human masters, since you know that you will receive an inheritance from the Lord as a reward. It is the Lord Christ you are serving."
Colossians 3:23-24

CHAPTER 4

INVEST YOUR TIME WISELY

***Invest Time in Yourself**
***Invest Time in Life Planning**
***Invest Time in People**

"In their hearts humans plan their course, but the Lord establishes their steps."
Proverbs 16:9

We don't need God to give us more hours in our day; we need to invest the time we do have in those areas which we most highly value.

People invest their money for a fruitful return on their dollar. Time, which is far more precious than money, should also be invested for fruitful return. Just spending or wasting time will not yield long-lasting results.

"Blessed are those who listen to Me,
watching daily at My doors,
waiting at My doorway.
For those who find Me find life
and receive favor from the Lord."
Proverbs 8:34-35

A good place to start investing your time is to look at the ideal life you have pictured and then prioritize your goals that you set forth for yourself, as we have discussed previously. By working diligently on your goals, you very well could end up with:

Marriages being strengthened
Children becoming responsible adults
Households being run well
Friendships developing and deepening
Communities benefitting

Think about it – how are you investing your time NOW to give fruitful return?

Now think about ways in which you would like to invest your time in the future.

"Busyness is not essentially wrong.
Frustration comes when our busyness is
not profitable."

A Mother's Time by Elise Arndt

INVEST TIME IN YOURSELF

Human beings are very complex. We are made up of spirit, soul and body. Each part must be cared for and nourished or a well-balanced life is not attainable. Often we get too busy and life becomes a vicious cycle which resembles a merry-go-round of work, eat and sleep. God created us for more than that!

Think about six activities that you enjoyed doing as a child.

Think about ten activities that you enjoy now.

Our interests should be *increasing* as we grow older. There are so many new, interesting and exciting things to learn and experience!

What do you see about your life now in regard to those two previous questions?

Eight Practical Steps to Invest in Yourself

How important is it to continue to develop personally? In a word, *very*! It is all too easy to get bogged down in the dailies. We tend to forget that we are unique with special interests and talents given us by our Creator. Our uniqueness, if it isn't nurtured, will wither and die. We will have buried who we are and the dreams we hold dear. What a loss of minutes, hours, days and years of our lives!

Here are some ideas to help you move forward in your own personal growth:

1. **Read, read, read**

Explore topics that interest you. There are how-to books on every subject imaginable. Libraries, bookstores and the Internet are treasure troves of knowledge.

2. **Network.**

Keep connected. Your life is probably full of a variety of people to enjoy and from whom you can learn – professional associates, neighbors, those in your community, parents of your children's friends and co-workers. You never know where a connection may lead.

3. **Volunteer**

This is an excellent way to explore new avenues, meet new people and be of service to your community – usually on your own terms. Many volunteer opportunities have led to exciting new careers.

4. **Upgrade your skills**

Whether you are a grandparent, parent, administrative assistant, nurse or _*fill in the blank*_, there is always room for growth and improvement. Putting it off only puts you further behind.

5. **Learn new skills**

Take time to decide what would bring you pleasure to learn. Writing? Photography? A new computer program? Rug braiding? Get started and see where it leads.

6. Keep physically fit

As we go from our 20s, to our 40s, 60s, and 80s, we will realize how important it is to stay fit for each season. We don't need to run marathons. Fitness is as simple as moving your body daily. Many of us have sedentary occupations so moving can only be beneficial. Try simply walking, stretching, and/or balance exercises. All are easy as we start slowly and build.

Don't forget to keep stress and anxiety at the minimum as much as possible because we know that prolonged stress affects our bodies – high blood sugar, being overweight, heart attacks and stroke. You can do certain things to protect yourself through the years!

7. Balance your nutrition

Food and drink are the nutritional elements which fuel our bodies. Be wise in your choices – moderation in all things is the key. Then make sure you are drinking liquids – preferably water.

I learned this the hard way. I had a job which did not even allow time for sips of water between phone calls coming in nor adequate restroom breaks. Thus, lack of water resulted in a urinary tract infection which led to an infection throughout my body and the need for an early retirement. I had planned to work until I was 70…but something as simple as not drinking enough water each day cut short my working years. Drink water! It's the healthiest thing you can drink.

8. Have some fun!

When we have fun, we cope better with stress which sets up protective mechanisms for better health all around. Sometimes we need to find some fun which is some alone time with hobbies, reading, walking or whatever is enjoyable to *you*. At other times, the fun we have can include others which gives us the benefit of social interaction.

Unfortunately, many of us have forgotten all about the fun aspects of life. Increasingly, experts are saying that midlife is where fun goes to die. Our lives are so structured and serious that "there is often no room for spontaneity," says Stuart Brown, MD, a professor emeritus of psychiatry at the University of California, San Diego, and president of the National Institute for Play. "You're probably responsible, a hard worker, a moral person, and very involved with taking care of kids, parents, other people. But when you're not experiencing playful moments, you're not honoring your own need for unfettered joy."

Investment in yourself can make dreams turn into reality. That's an excellent use of time!

Invest Time in Having a Mentor

It has been said that trees planted in a clearing of an old forest will grow more successfully than one planted in an open field by itself. It is believed that the roots of the newly planted tree are able to follow the intricate pathways created by former trees and thus embed themselves more deeply

We hear a great deal these days about being a mentor but when was the last time anyone encouraged you to become a mentee – the one who benefits from being mentored?

Think back to your childhood. Who were some of the people who had a positive influence on your life? Was it a teacher? An auntie? A neighbor? Your own mother or grandmother? Your father? All of us, no matter who we are, have had mentors along life's pathways.

Who are your mentors now? Is there anyone presently in your life who walks alongside you to encourage you in your day-to-day life? Or are you trying to walk alone, doing the best you can at home and/or at work?

What has changed you into a person who tries to go it alone? Do you consider yourself grown up now and no longer in need of someone to encourage you or teach and train you in areas where you need strengthening?

How much time and energy could you save if you would find someone to walk alongside you, sharing their treasures of experience, knowledge and wisdom? You could actually learn anything you set your heart to learn; that new program at work, photography, kayaking, a second language, making homemade soap, watercolor painting, writing or anything which is of interest to you.

Perhaps you have been trying to master these tasks on your own and can only get so far in reaching your goals. It may be time to consider finding a mentor to take you farther along the path.

Qualities to Seek in a Mentor

What are the qualities you should seek when you are searching for a mentor? Consider what a mentor should be:

* A person who cares about you
* One who is a good role model
* Someone you can trust

* Someone willing to give you the gift of their time
* A person knowledgeable in the areas in which you express interest
* Someone who is a good listener
* A person who is able to give you wise counsel
* One who offers support and encouragement
* A person who is able to correct your mistakes truthfully and kindly
* One who is excited to see you succeed

How to Find Your Mentor

Look around you. A person who could serve as your mentor probably doesn't have a big *mentor* sign emblazoned across their forehead. Your mentor is probably someone you already know who is quietly doing the work that must be done in this world and is doing it well.

Be creative in your search for a mentor. Mentors can be found in many places: they may be among your friends, neighbors, co-workers or family members. Perhaps there is a class being offered where you can be mentored by the instructor. Long distance mentoring, although not ideal, could take place via letter, phone conversations or even the Internet. If you find books which contain the wisdom and knowledge you need, sit at the author's feet, reading and learning all you can absorb.

Stages of Being Mentored

Now that you have decided that you want to be mentored and have chosen a mentor who has said yes, it's time to get down to work. The following comes next:
* Get together with your mentor and discuss what you would like to derive from your mentor/mentee relationship.
* Establish goals you, personally, would like to attain.
* Plan the steps needed to reach your goals.
* Determine how often you will meet and then stick to your commitment.
* Start progressing toward those goals, periodically re-evaluating your progress.

Your Responsibilities as a Mentee

Being mentored may be structured, such as learning a new software program step by step; or it may be non-structured such as learning carpentry work by working alongside someone. No matter what form your mentor/ mentee relationship takes, it remains your responsibility to communicate clearly your expectations of the relationship.
* Be a good listener.
* Submit yourself to your mentor's direction.
* Be consistent in striving to meet the goals you decided upon.
* Hold yourself accountable.

Thus, choose your mentor wisely, then commit yourself to a season of learning.

Plan for Closure

Your mentor/mentee relationship may not last forever. Don't, however, allow your relationship to fade away. Plan what will be done after you, the mentee, have accomplished your goals. Perhaps a deeper friendship is ahead!

Do you remember that newly planted tree whose roots were following pathways created by former trees? May you follow its example and find pathways for yourself to gain wisdom and knowledge from those who have walked those pathways before you.

Your Body's Rhythms

We also need to remember our body's natural rhythms which add to our complexity as human beings. We have seasonal, monthly and daily rhythms.

During what part of the day do you feel most alive?

Which season of the year do you find most enjoyable?

We need to love ourselves enough to listen to ourselves. Scripture tells us:

"Love the Lord your God with all your heart and with all your soul and with all your mind and with all your strength. The second is this: Love your neighbor as yourself. There is no commandment greater than these."

Mark 12:30-31

How do we love and listen to ourselves? The author, John Bradshaw, states this concept perfectly in his book *Creating Love*":

> "If you decide to love yourself, you will be willing to give yourself time and attention.... The work of love involves giving yourself time. How much time do you spend with yourself? Do you take time for proper rest and relaxation or do you drive yourself unmercifully.... If you're willing to love and accept yourself unconditionally, you will allow yourself time to just be. You will set aside times when there's nothing you have to do and nowhere you have to go. You will allow yourself solitude, a nourishing time of aloneness.... The work of love is the work of listening to yourself. You listen to yourself by monitoring your feelings needs and wants. You need to pay attention to yourself.... The work of paying attention to yourself requires discipline."

Of course, it is not meant that we become self-centered or a hypochondriac, centering all of our thoughts and activities on the self, but we do need to listen to ourselves. If we don't, we are going through life as if we were blind, deaf and paralyzed.

Do you fight what your body is telling you or do you try to listen and provide what is needed?

The Importance of a Day of Rest

Do you have the feeling that your work is never finished? As soon as you finish scrubbing the kitchen floor…again, someone spills pineapple juice in a sticky puddle right in the walkway. One task leads to another… and another…a never-ending circle. Your personal to do list, also, seems to grow longer, not shorter. If one item is crossed out, there are ten more to replace it. Weekends are full of chores that didn't get done during the week: laundry, yard cleanup, housecleaning. Even vacations, when squeezed in, aren't all that restful either. Family members want as much fun packed into it as possible. You know that you need a rest, but you wonder how you can possibly step off the merry-go-round of ceaseless activity to benefit from it. The rhythm of life has been lost.

Why We Don't Rest

As a culture, tremendous value is placed on accomplishments, hard driving success and endless to do lists. Little value is placed on a time of rest, a time of seeming lack of productivity; a quiet walk through the woods, a bedtime story read to a child or a leisurely bath. These activities aren't held in high esteem since they don't contribute anything to the gross national product or to your paycheck. Thus, when a rest is taken, guilt abounds.

Those people who are in the caring professions (nurses, doctors, teachers plus mothers and fathers especially) feel guilty if they aren't doing more and doing it better than it has ever been done before. Mothers and fathers, especially, are expected to be on duty 24 hours a day without a break in their parental responsibilities.

Why Rest Is Needed

Most of us believe that our energy is limitless, unending. Then one day we come down with the flu, our energy is gone and we realize how precious that commodity is.

Sabbath by Wayne Muller tells of studies conducted at the University of Arizona where it was discovered that there is a biological need for rest every seventh day. They also saw the evidence of the energizing value of rest. Failure to rest after six days of steady work was seen to lead to insomnia or sleepiness, hormonal imbalances, fatigue, irritability, organ stress and other increasingly serious physical and mental symptoms.

From these studies we can conclude that a day of rest is as necessary as oxygen for our body's well-being! Are we listening?

"In vain you rise early
and stay up late,
toiling for food to eat—
for He grants sleep to those he loves."
Psalm 127:2

What Is a Day of Rest?

In most of the world's ancient spiritual traditions, a Sabbath or day of rest isn't just a hint but is an admonishment. A day of rest is actual time which we set aside from the pursuits which keep us busy the other six days of the week. Jewish tradition encourages us to take a day which would include the following:

* Rest
* Reflection
* Rejuvenation
* Remembering
* Reverence

The Jewish Sabbath is an excellent example of what a day of rest should be. Whether the work is completed or not, all comes to a stop when the sun goes down on Friday night. For an entire 24 hours there is a different mindset. There is, in a very real sense, the admission that the Creator can run the universe without our help for one day. What a relief that could be for us! We could stop the endless tasks of everyday life and truly set aside a day for delight.

Another Culture's Story

Once, so the story is told, some South American natives were leading an expedition into the dense forests. Day after day they would walk tirelessly. On the seventh day, however, they stopped walking, made camp and refused to go any farther. When asked why, they explained they needed the time of rest so that their souls could catch up with them.

Wise people…may we take a lesson from their example.

How to Let Your Soul Catch Up

What are some activities you can incorporate into your day of rest to allow your soul to catch up? Think about these possibilities:

* Sleep as long as you want in the morning, allowing yourself to waken naturally without the aid of an alarm clock.

* Eat leisurely, healthy meals and snacks. Loosen up, just for one day, on the strict diet you have been trying to maintain.

* Unplug from the world of technology. Let the phone, texting, TV, and computer go on without you.

* Gather with friends just to enjoy one another's company.

* Let someone else do the cooking and clean up – order out or have a leisurely meal at a restaurant.

* Perform an act of kindness for someone else, visit someone who is ill or lonely.

* Gather to worship and for prayer.

* Enjoy the arts. Amble through an art gallery or try your own hand at watercolor, weaving, spinning, quilting, calligraphy….

* Write in your personal journal.

* Take a nap.

* Go for an extended walk with no destination in mind. Just enjoy the sights and sounds of nature.

* Keep silence.

* Putter around in your flowerbeds.

* Label your family photos, updating your albums or scrapbooks.

* Give thanks for the abundance you already possess.

You get the idea. Choose to do something you want to do for the sole purpose of being renewed and refreshed. Then when it is time for the next six days of your life, you will be ready and eager!

"...the seventh day is a sabbath to the Lord your God. On it you shall not do any work, neither you, nor your son or daughter, nor your male or female servant, nor your animals, nor any foreigner residing in your towns."
Exodus 20:10

What six things would you enjoy incorporating into your days off?

On a *day off,* many sleep their time away and feel groggy even when awake. Researchers have found that maintaining your regular sleep habits, even on weekends, keeps you functioning at your best. If you are tired, it has been found that a short 20 minute nap is more effective than a long one.

What are your usual bedtime and rising hours on weekdays, on Saturday, on Sunday?

As women, we sometimes think we are wasting precious time sleeping. We'd rather be DOING. But sleep has great benefits! To name just a few: our muscles rest, the heart rate slows, cells repair and replenish themselves and the brain integrates all of our hopes, fears and buried images. Sleep is NOT a waste of time!

If we women have a difficult time taking one day off per week, imagine taking a vacation.

Invest Time in Planning a Vacation

Vacations, no matter what type is chosen, should replenish your soul, refresh your spirit and renew your body.

What makes the difference between a vacation which renews us and one which adds stress to our lives? Wise planning and good time management skills are the magic ingredients for before and during the vacation. Don't forget, vacations are supposed to be *fun*!

Choose a Vacation Based on Your Needs

1. Try an At-Home Vacation. Vacations are a state of mind, not a destination. Being at home can have a restful effect. Read some books, putter around inside, take a walk, go out to dinner with friends.

2. Explore Day Trips. Go to the beach for the day, visit the local museum, enjoy the bird sanctuary, dress up for dinner and the theater. Then return to the comfort of your own home each evening.

3. Take a Weekend Get Away. This could be perfect for getting reacquainted with those important to you after a busy season.

4. Rediscover the Same Old Place. Try further exploration in a place you have been before. A resort you love or a family cabin may be calling your name.

5. Take a Cruise. Soak up some sunshine and enjoy being catered to from morning to night. Pretend it will last forever.

6. Book a Tour. Let someone else do the driving and join a bus tour. Let them plan the itinerary, reserve meals and take charge of the luggage.

7. Attend a Family Reunion. Reestablish contact with those you haven't seen in years or keep connected with those you saw last week. Family times together are priceless!

8. Think Educational. Many seminars and workshops include an extended time away. Learn and enjoy at the same time!

9. Travel by Train. What an adventure! See sights while eating and sleeping along the way.

10. Volunteer for Your Vacation. Use your time and energy to help others. Go on an archaeological dig, build a house, serve at your local hospital or hospice.

11. Enjoy the out-of-doors. Try some biking, golfing, sailing, surfing, hiking, fishing or camping. Sit under a tree, enjoy the view, read a book and listen to the birds.

12. Other Ideas: Research family history, experience Road Scholar, soak up solitude, exchange homes, discover going out of the country.

Do Your Vacation Planning Homework

Go online. Specific details about your destination are limitless – weather, prices, maps, photos, fares, local sights, restaurants and events.

Go to the library. Find books about your places of interest. Ask the reference librarian for help. Order books through inter-library loan.

Ask family and friends. If you want to vacation in an area new to you, get some input from those who have been there. They will give you the inside story about a place.

Get brochures. Send away for specific information utilizing the local Chamber of Commerce or places of interest.

Call a travel agent. Choose a person who will advise you wisely and be willing to do some comparison pricing and negotiating, looking out for your best interests.

Put it on Paper or Online

Set up an itinerary. Write out your plan so you will be able to visualize your entire vacation. Keep your schedule somewhat flexible. This is a vacation! Always have contingency plans in case any problems arise.

Make your reservations. Record your specific reservation and confirmation number in your itinerary. Don't forget to add the contact person's name.

Make a to-do list. Remember to include all pertinent items such as who will care for your pets, the plants and who will bring in the mail.

Make a to-pack list. Eliminate any last minute panic and keep adding to the list as you think of items to take with you.

When the planning portion of your vacation is complete, all that is left is the packing. Now go ahead...be replenished, refreshed and renewed.

Invest Time in Retirement Planning

Retirement may seem like it is *many* years away whether you have two or 25 more years to have a traditional job. Trust me, the years go by so fast that, when retirement arrives, one wonders *how* that happened. Thus, we must keep alert to the fact that retirement *will* arrive and it is best *now* to begin preparing for it.

Please know that there are many excellent books available about retirement planning, financial planning and estate planning so I will just touch on it briefly here. As the time to retire approaches, do your homework.

Also please realize that those things we did as a younger person, we will do similarly as a more mature person. Hopefully, when we are young, we will learn the lessons needed in each season of our lives, to walk in grace and beauty of spirit, soul and body.

Recently a friend asked me what she would be like when she is *old*. My answer was simple; you will be just more of who you are now. If you are calm and well organized, you will be that way then. If you are frazzled, disorganized and hurried as a younger person, you will be the same in the *golden years* which, sometimes, aren't very golden for a variety of reasons.

Retirement is strange. Sometimes it is well planned out and one steps smoothly from one chapter to another in life *or* retirement comes with a shock, as in my case.

One day I was putting in my 8 hours a day at work, being gone from home daily for 10 hours. Then one night I knew I was really sick! I hadn't felt well for weeks but being the Hurried Woman I am, I pushed through. That night I called the ambulance and decided I needed physical help *now*. I was sick. I just could *not* push through another day…or minute.

A simple urinary tract infection was missed by my doctor. When it was left untreated, it resulted in septicemia – an infection throughout my entire blood stream. My kidneys were shutting down. Next other organs would begin shutting down. I felt horrible!

After a four day hospital stay, I was released to go home on antibiotics; but things got worse and I ended up back in the hospital, unable to speak an intelligent word or think in any coherent way. Thankfully the Lord reversed things but ,after I went home again, it became increasingly clear that I would not be returning to work…ever. Too much damage had been done over the length of time it took them to find the problem and correct it, with more mistakes along the way.

So, sometimes we find ourselves landing in the retirement chapter of our lives more quickly than we thought. Thus, it is wise to look at it ahead of time.

What do YOU want your retirement years to look like, especially in regard to how you will use your time?

As a working adult, you will have gone from a structured time clock kind of existence to absolute freedom, 24/7.

What will you do with that freedom?

Will you fill it with classes, trips, lunches, grandchildren or will you find yourself at a loss as to what to do each day so you end up dong nothing?

Will you hop out of bed, eager for the day or will you find yourself sleeping and napping the day away?

Of course, when first retired, one will want to catch up on rest - as much as needed. Yet, when you find yourself well rested again, it will be time to slowly add some activity.

For me, I began a list years ahead of retirement time of those things I'd like to do or do more of. My list included: writing more, capturing more photos, having more time to read and explore ideas, keeping connected with family and friends, and more. Little did I know that I would need to refer to that list when I landed at home with a thud of ill health. I also needed to do a great deal of work to regain a semblance of a lifestyle now called my new normal. Then I could live out the list I'd been making for years.

After I settled into the retired life and began to feel better, one thing I noticed was that I brought my hurried lifestyle tendencies to retirement. I found myself wanting to do *everything* and do it *now.* Thus, I began pulling together all of the information I'd gathered through the years and have again been learning how to apply those principles to my life now. It is time to write this book which has been brewing for years.

Do you remember that I mentioned the *golden years* previously? We may envision those years as such but we could also, instead, have the *struggling to feel better years* with that *new normal.* Due to physical problems as we get older, we may have to slow down. Then we find that the hours we spent working are now spent on health issues – doctors appointments, medications and charts to keep them all straight, nutritional changes, exercising for strength and balance…it's a different time of our lives. It seems like the chapter where we found ourselves caring for a newborn is now spent caring for *ourselves* to attain and maintain our lives. Of course we may land in retirement, totally healthy but, if not, we need to learn to accept our limitations and learn to live within them, not fighting against them. It would be time to learn how we can grow older with grace -- God's grace. It's finally time to learn to take care of ourselves if we've never done that before…ever.

Don't Forget to Have Some Fun!

One thing we, as Hurried Women need to do daily, is to find something fun to do. We have lived too long in the seriousness of caring for others, working hard at everything we set our hands to do, also neglecting ourselves. Now, especially, it is time to apply all of the principles we've learned here:

* To step off the merry-go-round of life and find out your own best life. It is all too easy to fall into others' expectations of us now that we are retired. What does *God* have for *you* to do in this new season? Do you have purpose in your life and in each day?

* To simplify our activities, relationships and possessions so we can walk ahead freely. We don't want to be encumbered by too many and too much. In fact, when I was newly retired, I spent some time cleaning out drawers and closets – I'd been too busy working to keep things as simple and as orderly as I'd wanted.

* To specialize in those things we really want to do because, at the end of our lives, we want our lives to count. There is so much good we can do in the world and in our families!

* To delegate tasks which we no longer want to do or possibly can not do. Maybe the gardening, which you once enjoyed, needs to be delegated now. For me, I hated giving up getting my hands in the dirt but I'm perfectly content with container gardening – easy to reach and enjoy.

* To maintain balance in every area of our lives is *so* important as we grow older. Hopefully, we will also grow wiser with the years.

Let's practice good time and space management principles NOW and we will reap the benefits!

INVEST TIME IN LIFE PLANNING

One sure way to invest your time wisely is to spend your time prayerfully planning – your days, weeks, months and lives.

Our society is action oriented. It leads us to believe that if we aren't doing something then we must not be doing anything. What about 'think' time, prayer time, planning time? All of that time is quiet and non-active time but worth far more than running here and there accomplishing only the running part. Research studies show that the amount of time we spend planning is in direct proportion to the amount of time we save.

For example, if we run out of the door to do errands without a plan, we forget to do some things, double back and forth trying to get everything accomplished. With a well thought-through plan, however, all is done in an efficient, sane manner. The same can be said for life – with a well thought out plan (you have that with your list of ideals and prioritized goals) you know where you are headed and what to do to get there.

How much time do you spend in planning?

What technique do you use – personal planner, to do lists, calendar, an online planner?

Are you happy with your planning techniques? If not, what can you change?

If you decide to use a planner in your computer, make sure it is easy and functional.

If you decide to use a paper planner, a good one need not cost a great deal of money. You can purchase a small three ring binder, cut 81/2 X 11 inch sheets of paper in half for filler and purchase some subject dividers.

The following is what I use in my planner. It may give you some ideas to help you keep things all in one place to make life easier. The divisions reflect my life.

Calendar for the month
To-Do List for the day/month
Prayer list
Letters or emails to write
Birthdays
Holiday card list
Borrowed books (from whom and when)

Books loaned out to others (to whom and when)
Good books (books I'd like to read someday)
Quotes (poems, thoughts)
Work related items
Projects (amount of fabric, measurements)

Master grocery list

Recipes to try and a reminder of which ones are successful to repeat

Planners are fun to custom design and to use!

A Good Planner Should Be:

Functional

If you use a planner, you won't have scraps of paper throughout the house with a lot of dashing around trying to find the misplaced information. All information is in one spot in your planner and that means your mind can stay free to be the creative tool it was meant to be, not crammed with the miscellaneous details of life.

A fancy big planner on paper or online is no good to us unless we are able to use it to make life *easier.* If your planner (or computer program) is so complex that it takes too much time and energy to use or if you can't find anything in it easily, you are better off not using one at all. Keep it simple and functional. Do some research and see what apps are available to make it easy.

With goals and deadlines visible.

Long term and short term daily goals can be listed and prioritized with a small square box in front of each item.

When the task is completed, the box is filled in with a pen. That way, at a glance, you can see what has been completed and what still needs to be completed.

I also use a personal calendar. For each item, I include all of the pertinent details - where, time, what to bring. If an invitation is received, it can be filed away but, if lost, all of the information is on the calendar.

Many families keep a family calendar, color coded for each person's activities. That way nothing is forgotten and each person, at a glance, can see what is happening with the family as a whole. As a parent, the busyness can be monitored so there still remains family time.

One family I know recently looked at their calendar for the summer and realized that each of them and all of them were so busy, there was no time to enjoy the summer. Changes were made before the summer even began.

If you choose to use an online planner, an important thing to remember is that, no matter what type of planner you use, organizing is not the goal. It is just a method to use to attain a well balanced life.

Let's not become a slave to a calendar, to do list or method; let them serve *you.*

INVEST TIME IN PEOPLE

Quality relationships should be a prime focus in our lives. After all, we DO have family and friends. We need to, on a daily basis, build and replenish our relationships with others.

Please remember, as stated previously, that a woman doesn't have to work outside the home to be absent. She can be home full time and still stay too busy, sometimes with very legitimate activities, to pay attention to her family. She may be physically present but emotionally absent.

In her book *Home by Choice: Facing the Affects of a Mother's Absence*, Brenda Hunter contends that:

> "A child internalizes a sense of 'home' or an abiding sense of homelessness based on those earliest parental attachments, and that the mother is central to this process. If a mother is often absent or emotionally inaccessible, a child may suffer profoundly."

Are *your* children homeless?

Is *your* spouse homeless?

Are *you* homeless?

Almost anyone can do the work a mother does. What cannot be replaced is who she is while she lovingly does that work for her family.

Attributes Needed

In order to invest time in people, may I suggest three attributes which are important:

1. Be a good listener.
Do you find yourself buzzing around as your family and co-workers talk to you on the run? A good listener STOPS and LISTENS while establishing eye contact.

Are you a good listener or do you need to practice listening?

2. Be a creator of good memories with family and friends.
Have fun together. Go out to dinner. Fly a kite. Be silly. Romp in the snow. Laugh together. Plant flowers. Read books together. Jump in the autumn leaves. Life can be serious business but it should also be a time of enjoying one another in delight.

Think of six things you would like to do with your family and friends to create some good memories.

3. Train your children to become responsible adults.
This is a definite wise investment of your time! (More about this in a subsequent chapter.) We need to teach our children to learn to live in the real world where they don't always *get their way,* We also need to learn not to cater to a child's every whim. We need to carve out time for an adult life and conversation.

Yes, good parenting is a balancing act! But we can do it, one decision at a time. Can you do it?

Try Negotiating Not Nagging

Do you find yourself nagging from morning to night? Try negotiation in some areas but, for children, they also need to obey what they are told to do…the first time. That is NOT negotiable.

What, specifically, is negotiating? To negotiate means "to confer, bargain or discuss with a view to reaching an agreement".

How to Negotiate

Let's take the negotiating process step by step to learn how best to accomplish your goals:

1. Recognize there is a problem.

Take a 24 hour span of time this week and listen to yourself. Are you constantly giving orders, demanding and nagging?

Keep a time log for a week of household responsibilities and who does them to get a clear picture of why you feel so stressed.

2. Establish rapport with family members.

Instead of jumping right in to correct the problem, step back, lighten up and have some fun.

Also, make sure you are already recognizing and showing your appreciation for all of the *right* things your spouse and children do. Family members thrive in a positive, respectful atmosphere.

3. Negotiate a plan with family members.

Household tasks are everyone's responsibility, not just the woman's. Therefore, let each family member be a part of the negotiating team. They may come up with some solutions you never thought about.

Be specific about what you see and feel in regard to an imbalance of household chores. The plain facts in the form of your time log could go a long way toward negotiating solutions.

4. Let it go.

Once it has been decided that a task is the responsibility of someone else, it is time to take hands off. That may be difficult at first, but to continue nagging only sets up the negative communication cycle again. Of course, the tasks must still be completed on time and in the proper manner but a healthy delegation of responsibility is good for everyone. (More about delegation later.)

5. Hire it done.

If no one in the family has the time, the inclination or the skills to do a specific task such as cutting up a fallen tree, no amount of nagging will get the job done. Good negotiators will recognize when outside help is needed and will take appropriate action.

6. Renegotiate if there is a change.

If you find you've added a part-time job, full-time job or if it is time to be retired, it is definitely time to re-negotiate household responsibilities. Or perhaps your spouse has a stretch of time when the hours at work increase – be flexible so everyone can pitch in to cover for each other. Mutual cooperation should be the character of any family.

Invest in Setting Time Boundaries

Are you able to recognize when your time boundaries are being violated? Ask yourself the following questions:

* Do I try to do too much for others?

* Do I ignore my own needs?

* Do I continue to push myself beyond my limits day after day?

* Do I use caffeine and/or sugar and energy drinks to keep going?

* Do I refuse to rest when I am tired?

* Do I neglect to exercise?

* Do I deprive myself of quiet and solitude?

* Do I consistently, night after night, try to get away with the minimum hours of sleep?

If you answered yes to any of these questions, you may want to evaluate your time boundaries.

1. What Are Time Boundaries?

Time boundaries are protective fences we place around ourselves and the hours in our day to:
* Bring order to our lives
* Gain a clearer sense of who we are
* Determine how we will treat ourselves and be treated by others.

2. The Importance of Establishing Time Boundaries

Each of us has been given 24/7 by our Creator in which to live. If we are wise, we will realize that, for our own sakes and for the sake those whom we love, we must protect the time we have been given, making sure we live a balanced, well-paced life.

3. What Happens Without Time Boundaries

In order to gain a clearer understanding of the importance of time boundaries, let's consider your days. Is your life well ordered and sanely paced or are you pulled in a thousand directions by too many commitments, too many responsibilities and too little time to fit everything in?

4. Identify Problem Areas

If you are being pulled in a thousand directions, it is time to stop and identify those problem areas in your life. That's where a time log can come in handy. Too often we just push *automatic* and run through our days. Let's be mindful about what we are doing and what is going on around us.

5. Establish Your Time Boundaries

Establishing boundaries of any kind is difficult, especially time boundaries. Since you know their importance, however, you must make a plan to:

* Allow the time you need for proper rest and sleep

* Protect your meal times allowing time to prepare and partake of nutritious meals

* Avoid consuming sugar, caffeine and other stimulants to keep going

* Recognize the importance of exercise and actually carve out the time to do it!

* Stop trying to do too much!

6. Evaluate Your Progress

When you try to establish time boundaries, the challenges often get bigger. It seems everyone in the world wants MORE of your time. Stand firm in your decisions to protect what you know to be right for you and your loved ones.

7. Make Adjustments

Flexibility is needed as special circumstances and needs arise. Make the adjustments and keep moving toward your goal of managed time boundaries.

The time boundaries you have established must be maintained for your protection. Rely on them and live within them. You will walk with confidence and with a lighter step.

Invest Time in Making the Most of Meetings

A great way to practice setting time boundaries is with the vast number of meetings we are called upon to attend.

Meetings in our society today are prevalent. They threaten to take up every spare moment we have. Meetings at work, at our child's school, at our place of worship and meetings for our volunteer commitments crowd our precious moments.

Productive meetings can give a sense of accomplishment. Poorly run meetings which are non-productive, however, lead to feelings of frustration for everyone involved.

If we aren't wise, we will be robbed of precious minutes, hours and days as we sit through one meeting after another, never accomplishing what we want to do and should be doing.

The following are some tips which may be helpful whether you attend or conduct a meeting.

If You Attend a Meeting

Obtain a copy of the agenda before the meeting.

1. **Look over what will be discussed.** Then you will be able to ask pertinent questions and/or make appropriate, brief comments. Perhaps your presence at the meeting isn't necessary.

2. **Look at your options.** Be wise in the use of your time! You may need to attend only that portion of the meeting which applies to you. Or you may be able to send a written report instead of being present.

3. **Set clear goals.** Decide what you would like to derive from or contribute to a particular meeting.

4. **Do your part well.** If you have a specific report or presentation to give, do so in a well organized, concise manner. If you have questions, get to the point quickly.

5. **Take notes.** However brief, use key words to help you remember what was discussed. Put a huge colorful star by any item which calls for action on your part.

6. Transfer information. If another meeting has been called, immediately mark the date, time and location on your calendar. If you have placed stars by items for which you are responsible, enter them on your to-do list.

7. File your agenda and notes. Set up a file and place all pertinent meeting information in it. If called upon to remember something discussed, it will be at your fingertips.

If You Conduct a Meeting

1. Decide if a meeting is necessary. Is it possible to conduct the needed business via a simple telephone call, conference call, e-mail, letter, memo or fax?

2. Determine the purpose of the meeting. Is the meeting to gather or share information, aid in decision making or to train others? Without a purpose, a meeting will go nowhere, fast.

3. Include only key people. Choose only those key people who need to be present. Inform each if you want them to give a presentation, being specific as to content and time limit.

4. Schedule the meeting. Choose a date, time and location which will cause the least interruption in the normal flow of work and life.

5. Think of the comfort of the participants. Are there adequate tables, chairs, fresh air flow and lighting in your meeting room? Is the temperature comfortable? Is water available? Will everyone be able to hear you and each other?

6. Be prepared. If your speaking skills are rusty, take a public speaking class or join a local branch of Toastmasters to boost your confidence. If you have graphics to present, make sure they are of good quality and that the presentation process flows smoothly.

7. Start promptly. If latecomers arrive, do not repeat information, wasting your time and the time of those who were prompt. Just keep moving ahead with your presentation.

8. Lay the ground rules. Let participants know that you will be closely following the agenda.

9. Designate someone to take notes and to type minutes. Taking notes and filing minutes for the meeting gives value to what is done. There will be an ongoing record of what was discussed and the resolution of each matter.

10. Stick to the agenda. The ideal situation is to put the agenda into the hands of each participant a few days ahead of time. Have fresh copies available at the time the meeting begins.

11. Summarize the highlights. At the end of the meeting, briefly summarize key points. Repeat any follow-up action needed.

12. Thank those who attended. Let the participants know that you appreciate them and their input.

13. Announce the next meeting. If a follow-up meeting is necessary, let the participants know at that time. They can enter the date, time and location on their calendars immediately. Of course, a reminder will be needed before the next meeting.

14. End on time. Everyone will be grateful to you when the meeting flows smoothly and ends as planned.

Now that you have some tips for attending or conducting a meeting, hopefully you will never look at a meeting in the same way again. Let's aim for productive meetings which give everyone involved a sense of accomplishment.

Time Investment Questions to Ask Yourself

There are three important questions you can ask yourself when you are faced with the multitude of choices facing you. Don't forget what you pictured your ideal life to be and the goals you have set for yourself.

1. Is this something I want to invest my time doing? When compared with all of your other tasks you do or the tasks you'd *like* to do, how does this request measure up?

2. Is this something that counts for me, for my family and the people who are important to me?

Too often we are asked to do more busy work. None of us needs more busy work.

3. What are my *options*?
You may choose not to do the requested task, you may choose to do a portion of the task or you may choose to do it in your own way. We do have options!

Think about six ways you could invest your time more wisely now.

Just remember that we don't want to sacrifice our lives to the tyranny of the urgent. We must live out well planned lives, as much as possible, since we only have one life to live. Make it count!

CHAPTER 5

LEARN TO DELEGATE RESPONSIBILITY!

– What is Delegation?
– Why We Don't Delegate
– Tasks We Can Delegate at Home and at Work
– The Importance of Delegating
– How to Delegate Responsibility
– Your Child and Delegation

Although it takes time initially to delegate responsibility, in the long run it will save time. The activities of daily living in a household or office are parceled out so that everyone works together to ensure a smoothly flowing home or office.

A century ago, all family members had to work together just to survive. From plowing, planting, harvesting, spinning, weaving and sewing, everybody pitched in and did their share of the work at the level at which they were capable. The children, adults and grandparents worked together for the common goal of survival.

In today's society, everyone rushes out the door to his or her own pursuits leaving breakfast dishes undone and beds unmade. Parents find themselves staying up late night after night to finish one more load of laundry, fix one more broken screen, unload the dishwasher, prepare clothes for the following day, pack lunches. If both parents work outside of the home, the tasks are multiplied even more. They feel like they need ten more sets of hands to complete all that needs to be done.

At work, there are phone calls, reports, meetings and an endless array of tasks to do each day. The day flies by and one senses that almost nothing was accomplished.

What is the solution? Delegation of responsibility!

Research has shown that if we learn how to delegate and practice delegation, we would be able to accomplish more each day!

What is Delegation?

To appoint and assign responsibility is to delegate. We often don't delegate even one small task as we try to do it all ourselves and then complain about how much we have to do.

Delegation of tasks within the family helps bring the family *home* again as they work together to survive in this busy world. In the office, it is called team building – working together. Children and adults, alike, feel a part of something larger than themselves when work is shared!

By delegating increasingly more difficult and complex tasks over the years from toddlerhood to the young adult years, our children are learning skills they will need for the rest of their lives. In the office, a newbie is taught the basics and an increasing number of tasks are delegated as skill levels rise. The same principles of delegation apply at home and at work.

Do you think that you are delegating appropriately at home?

Are you delegating at work?

Why We Don't Delegate

According to James M. Jenks and John M. Kelly in the book, *Don't Do, Delegate!,* the following are some excuses we use when we fail to delegate responsibility at home and at work:

* I can do it better.
* I can do it correctly.
* I want to keep it simple.
* I want to keep my hand in.
* I want the credit.
* I'm afraid it will fail if I don't do it.
* I don't want to appear lazy.
* I'm not a tyrant.

Notice that the first word in each excuse is the word "I". We, for whatever reasons, want to do everything ourselves. Perhaps we fear that the loss of control may result in something terrible happening. Why not be brave . . . consider delegating and become more effective!

Why aren't *you* delegating?

Tasks we can Delegate - at Home and at Work

1. Routine Work: Our time is often filled with routine work which could be done by someone else. Home examples: dusting, washing dishes. Office example: filing.

2. Necessary Work: At home and at work, there are many necessary tasks, yet do we need to be the ones to do them all? Home example: feeding the pets. Office example: telephone calls to verify appointments.

3. Trivial Work: Many of our tasks seem trivial but are very important for the smooth running of a household or office. Some can be delegated. Home example: putting silverware away. Office example: opening mail.

4. Specialty Work: Why do we insist on doing tasks which the experts can do in a more time-efficient manner? Sometimes it is more cost effective to hire work done. Home example: carpet cleaning. Office example: tax preparation (if you own your own business).

5. Chores: This group of activities includes all of those tasks which are that, a real *chore* for us to do. There is no need to feel guilty passing a chore along to someone else. That person may thoroughly enjoy it. Home examples: wash the car, mow the lawn. Office example: make the coffee.

The Importance of Delegating

Here are some excellent reasons to delegate:

1. Multiplies your productivity.
2. Sets your time free to do other meaningful tasks.
3. Opens communication with others as you work together.
4. Fosters a sense of teamwork.

How to Delegate Responsibility

The following principles can be applied as we learn how to delegate:

1. First, determine what tasks you want to delegate. Choose just one task you can think of for a start.

2. Second, determine to whom the task will be delegated. This will require knowing your designated worker and his or her abilities.
To whom will you delegate that task?

3. Third, determine how you want the task done.
Even though a task is delegated, it is still your responsibility to see that it is accomplished how you want it to be done. Have you factored in the time needed to plan how to delegate and follow-up to see it was done as you wanted?

4. Fourth, determine when you want the task completed. An open ended request is not delegation. Be specific! Give a deadline.

How Much Responsibility is Right for YOUR Child?

"It is so much easier to do it myself," we wail as we empty the dishwasher before we fall into bed at night, thoroughly exhausted.

Whether we work in an office full-time or at home, we try to do it all….for everyone. As we become increasingly exhausted, resentment begins to build toward the very ones we are tying to serve.

Why do we do this to ourselves? Do we really believe that it's easier to do everything ourselves? Whatever the reason, the end result is always the same: an exhausted person trying to do too much.

What is the solution?

If children are still living at home, they can be one of the most precious resources for help. All that is needed is to invest time in their training.

Your Child and Delegation

"Start children off on the way they should go, and even when they are old they will not turn from it."
Proverbs 22:6

The age and maturity level of each child must be considered before any new task is taught. For example, a three-year-old can be taught to put silverware away but shouldn't be expected to clean a bathroom using dangerous cleaning products.

Our child's previous experience and training should be kept in mind, also. If the child is already capable of making his bed daily, perhaps he is ready for the next level of activity – that of changing the bedding on laundry day.

Now look at the child's needs and desires. A two-year-old usually needs to be near his mother so he follows the mother around trying to *help* dust. A wise parent will take advantage of this window of opportunity and give some basic dusting instructions and provide the child with his very own dust cloth. You may never have to dust again!

Keep in mind the child's intelligence and aptitude. We cannot expect our children to perform tasks which are beyond their abilities. It will only discourage them.

How to Train a Child

The following nine principles may be of help:

1. Break the job into small parts.
A verbal order to "Clean up your room!" may be too overwhelming to a child. However, a checklist with specific tasks listed in words or pictures may get the job done. For example, a partial list may look like this:
* Pick up all the toys from the floor.
* Place toys in the toy box.
* Replace all books neatly on the bookshelf

2. Use clear, simple instructions.
Note in the example above that nothing is taken for granted. A child may pick up the toys but unless clear, simple instructions of expectations are given, the toys may be thrown in a closet instead of where thy were intended to go.

3. Provide the necessary equipment.

Doing any job is more difficult and time consuming if it takes five minutes to assemble the equipment each time the job is to be performed. Handy little carry-alls could contain needed equipment for the job and would certainly bring pleasure to a child doing his own *work*.

4. Express a positive attitude toward work.

Are we good models of behavior when it comes to household chores? If we expect our children to have a positive attitude about work, we need to model that behavior for them.

5. Teach step by step.

Don't assume the child knows how. Even though a child has watched the kitchen counter being cleaned a million times, that does not mean that the child knows how. Start from the assumption that the child knows nothing about doing a task and build from there.

6. Keep in mind the child's learning style while teaching.

Each child needs to be taught in a manner in which he or she can learn a task and complete it successfully. If the child is a visual learner, it would be important to show how the task is done while explaining. A written list of instructions for each job may be helpful, also. Find out your child's learning style and training becomes easier. An excellent source is *In Their Own Way* by Thomas Armstrong which talks about learning styles of each child. Also an excellent book for parents is *401 Ways to Get Your Kids to Work at Home* by Bonnie McCullough and Susan Mason.

7. Stay with the child for success.
Over a period of time, stay with the child three times until the task is completed properly, insisting on proper performance. Children love to *get away with* less than is expected – it is human nature. However, our insistence on proper performance will instill habits which will be of value for a lifetime.

8. Say two or more positive things.
Ninety-nine things can be right about a task performed by our children but why is it human beings, especially parents, find that one thing that wasn't done just right? Actively look for the good and then say something positive!

9. Keep work periods short and successful.
Take time to plan training sessions, enjoy the process and rejoice with the child over the end result.

In relation to delegating to children or adults, *remember*:

We can expect certain standards of work when we delegate to others, but it is what we INSPECT that ensures the job gets done as we want and need it done!

Also, in regard to delegating to others, watch out for passive rebellion. We all know what active rebellion looks like: "No, I won't do it". Most people, young and old, won't come right out and say it but they certainly may let their displeasure be known with passive rebellion – taking his or her own sweet time by dawdling over it all, sulking, whining, ignoring, being disrespectful, muttering under one's breath, repeatedly forgetting, glaring, rolling the eyes....these are all subtle ways to undermine what you are trying to accomplish – delegation to get the work done.

Life and work can become so much more enjoyable when we work together!

Helping Your Child With Homework

When school days begin for your children each year, you may find that your busy schedule is busier than ever. You work hard all day at home or at the office. By evening you are tired! How will you find the time and energy to help your children with their homework, baths and reading together at bedtime?

Although your child will be expected to do homework on her own, good time management skills on your part can help keep life flowing in an orderly manner for everyone.

Helpful Tips to Get the Job Done:

1. Have a positive attitude toward learning.
From birth onward, you have been your child's primary teacher. When school days arrive each year, your child will want to continue to share her new experiences with you. Having a positive attitude toward your child's school, her teacher and any assigned homework will speak volumes in encouraging your child to continue the learning process.

2. Find out the teacher's homework expectations.
As soon as the school year begins, find out what your child's teacher expects. How much time, approximately, should be spent on homework nightly? What subjects will

be covered on specific nights? Will homework be given over weekends? Will there be any long term projects? Is it easy to connect with the teacher with any questions?

3. Establish a family calendar.
Posted where everyone in the family can see it, a calendar lets you know who is going where and when. What a good way to discover if your child's (and your family's) life is so full of commitments so that homework can't be scheduled.

4. Maintain a consistent schedule.
Children thrive and planning time for homework is easier when their schedules are somewhat predictable and constant.

5. Provide proper nourishment and rest.
Children use a tremendous amount of energy in their work and play. If not well rested and nourished properly, ill health, a dimming of intellect and poor school performance result.

6. Allow time to *chill out* after school.
After being in a room full of children all day, your child probably will need some down time once she has arrived home. A snack and an attentive ear from mom to hear the happenings of the day would probably be welcome. What a perfect time to review backpack contents, including assigned homework.

7. Designate a specific time for daily homework.
Just like adults, our children have biological clocks, too. What is your child's best personal time for homework? Does she enjoy doing homework as soon as she hits the

door after school? Or would she rather have a snack first? Or does your child prefer to do homework after dinner when the day begins to wind down?

8. Designate a special homework place.
Let your child have some input. She may work best at the dining room table in the midst of family activity. Or she may prefer to work in her bedroom. Don't forget to provide the necessary supplies – paper, pencils, pens and proper lighting.

9. Take advantage of modern technology.
If you or your child is unsure of the homework assignment, call your child's homework hotline if one is available. Some schools now post information on the Internet to keep parents informed.

10. Expect and inspect.
Expect the best from your child. Inspect in a kindly manner. After all, as parents we are ultimately responsible for the education of our children.

11. Give rewards.
When homework is completed neatly and in a timely manner, some excellent rewards could be free time, playing a board game together, a family movie with a popcorn snack or an extra book read at bedtime. We are never too old to have a story read to us.

12. Teach your child time management skills.
If a long term project is assigned, you can encourage your child to break the project into smaller jobs, each with a

mini-deadline so that all is completed in a timely, organized fashion.

13. Plan for the next day.
Have your child set aside homework, schoolbooks, clothes, shoes and socks the night before to prevent a stressful morning.

There, you've done it! Using good time management skills, you have a plan for establishing a successful homework routine. That means success for your child and for you!

Overscheduled Children

Here are four questions to ask yourself to help determine if you may be allowing your children's days to be overscheduled:

1. Are you afraid that your children will become bored (oh, there's that terrible word) so you keep their days packed with activities?

2. Do you emphasize educational activities to the extent that every moment is filled with school and structured enrichment activities?

3. Have you forgotten that play is a child's work, and that children have tremendous tasks ahead of them from birth onward to learn about the world in which they live?

4. Have you, as an adult, overscheduled your life so that your children just tag along for the hurried ride, learning from you that an overscheduled calendar is normal?

The Dangers of Overscheduling Children

Even though our children have a great deal of energy, they cannot keep up with an overscheduled, hurried pace for an extended period of time. Researchers have found that children who are subjected to a stressful lifestyle become restless, irritable, depressed and have an altered attention span. Furthermore, when these patterns are established in childhood, they carry over into adulthood.

With the availability of cell phones and technical devices of all kinds, it is more important than ever not to allow our children to become overscheduled with 24/7 texting, calling, and emailing. It's an easy solution – turn off the devices so that family meal time can't be interrupted. Remember that a good night's sleep is a priority. Also, there needs to be time for some out-of-doors non-scheduled freedom.

What We Can Do to Help Our Children

Here are simple ways in which you as a parent can protect your children from over-scheduled days now and in the future:

*** Remember, childhood should be at an unhurried pace.**

Encourage your children to enjoy some of the activities which were enjoyed in simpler days long ago; a bike ride around the neighborhood, flying a kite, resting in a hammock, watching the clouds fly by, collecting fireflies, plunking on a piano just for fun, playing jump rope and jacks or planting a garden in a special spot.

*** Teach your children good time management skills starting in babyhood.**

Show your child that there is an orderly progression to each day – meal time, play time, nap time, picking up toys time, bath time, story time and bedtime. As we show a child that there is an ebb and flow to their days, without an abundance of too many scheduled activities, this concept will carry on into teen years and adulthood.

*** Realize that a child's day is packed with structured learning in school.**

Give them the freedom of unstructured play during non-school hours.

*** Decide to ride out any initial exclamations of "I'm bored!" during unstructured play times.**

Researchers have found that if given free time and space, children will fill that time with activities which interest them. Parental suggestions, however, may help to get their creative juices flowing once again.

*** Give your children opportunities to explore areas of interest, even if those interests change weekly.**

Try to avoid finding structured classes for every passing interest; give them the freedom to explore.

*** Recognize that children's play is their work.**

Children have a tremendous amount to learn in order to mature into adults. Not only is there language to learn but reading and calculating numbers. They also must learn how to get along with the people in their world. A great deal of this learning is through play, pure and simple play. Don't deprive them of it!

*** Limit extracurricular activities to what is manageable for each child's age and energy level.**

Sure, your children may balk at activity limitations, but that is to be expected. In the long run, however, the child will be healthier and happier physically and emotionally as you help them wisely choose between the overabundance of possibilities.

*** Shorten your own to-do list.**

Be a good role model for your children. If you are overscheduled, your children will think that is how they are to live, too.

*** Slow your pace.**

Yes, our lives are busy but if we keep to a slower pace doing those things which need to be done, everyone in the family will benefit, including you.

*** Young adult children.**

By the time children have grown and gone off to college or out into the working world, they will hopefully have learned good time management habits from you. It's important, however, to keep a close watch on teens and young adults. As they enter the world where they have more freedom, we all know there are pitfalls – too much stress, too little sleep, partying, drinking, drugs… and the list goes on. Be watchful, parent; your job as a parent does not end in the teen years. We all know the pitfalls of drinking, drugs and partying. For most of us, we found that the need for good parenting *increased* as the years have gone by -– even with adult 'children'.

Let's allow time and space for our children to have a full and wholesome childhood. As a parent, that is a challenge but also a privilege.

CHAPTER 6

MAINTAIN YOUR BALANCE

Strive for Excellence Not Perfection

Too often we hurry through our lives because we don't think we are *good enough*. Thus we keep working harder and harder so that we can be perfect.

What is perfectionism? It can be defined as a tendency to set extremely high standards and to be dissatisfied with anything less than perfection.

Researchers are still unsure whether perfectionism is due to learned behavior from parents who never said "good enough", or if certain people are genetically predisposed to become perfectionists. No matter the cause, the results can be devastating.

What a burden we place on ourselves when we have such unrealistic expectations. We end up drowning in deadlines and details as we try to keep our life in perfect order. Trying to be perfect becomes a waste of our time, crippling us with anxiety, self-doubt, frustration and criticism of ourselves and others.

When will we realize that only the Creator is perfect? We are human, full of imperfections. There is nothing wrong with trying to do the best we can at home and work. The problem comes when we can't tolerate failure, continually striving for perfection.

Perhaps it is time to re-think our priorities in life. Instead of striving for perfection, we can strive for excellence.

What is excellence?

We can view excellence as doing the best job we can do in each area of our lives. Not perfectly, but the best.

How can we strive for excellence? Consider the following:

1. **Become aware of the problem.**
Take time to reflect on your life. If you see a tendency toward perfectionism in any area, decide to take action in the direction of excellence, not perfection.

2. Establish your own values.
Set aside all of the musts, shoulds and oughts. Your life may not be perfect but if it satisfies you and God is pleased, that's what counts.

3. Enjoy the process.
Yes, one of our goals may be to have dinner on the table by 6 p.m. but enjoy the process – cutting the vegetables, setting the table with good dinnerware, arranging candles and fresh flowers as a centerpiece. Dinner can be served

with a creative, loving touch, the entire process bringing you joy.

4. Delegate tasks to others.
Whether at home or at work, allow others to share some of the responsibility. Keep a hands-off attitude and cultivate gratitude in your heart and on your lips for the help given.

5. Talk to yourself in positive terms.
Be kind to yourself. Instead of telling yourself, "You blew it again!" tell yourself, "Good job, keep up the good work!" You will probably find yourself becoming more positive toward those around you, too.

6. Declare, "Good enough!"
When you have achieved your aim, positively declare it and yourself, "Good enough!" with an exclamation of joy.

May we pursue excellence instead of perfection. May the words "Good Enough" ring loudly and clearly in our lives.

I wish I could wave a magic wand over you and your life so that you could magically maintain your balance day by day. However, there is no special formula, only day by day discipline applying the principles given and doing what works for YOU.

You have worked really hard as you've read through this book and have begun thinking about how to put the principles into practice. I applaud you!

You have stepped off the merry-go-round and, hopefully, have gained some new perspectives concerning where you are and where you want to go in your life's journey.

We have discussed simplifying activities by learning to say NO to too many and too much. Plus, we have discussed simplifying your environment as you declutter. We discussed simplifying your relationships, also. All of this will take time and practice.

You've learned about specializing in this season of your life and have begun picturing what your life's ideals looks like. Goals are being set and priorities established. This, too, will take time.

We've discussed investing time in yourself, in quality relationships and investing time in the activities you value most highly.

We also extensively discussed why we need to delegate and how to do it.

You have learned a great deal, hopefully, and have attained the beginnings of a balanced life. It will take a lifetime of practice to attain balance and to maintain it. With each season of your life, new challenges present themselves.

Now you can picture yourself walking (not running) through your days, enjoying your life. You never seem in a hurry because your days are well thought out and planned. You are living fully in the present, not rushing ahead in thought and actions to the future. You take time for yourself because you know that only then can you live at your best. You use your time wisely on the things which you value, making sure that people come before possessions. You value your past, even the mistakes, knowing that you are continually learning and growing. You are content with the simple pleasures of life, not needing more possessions or activities to be fulfilled. Quite a picture, isn't it? It is a picture of who you are becoming as you apply the principles here…again and again.

Enjoy your life! God created you to enjoy it and to give Him the glory!

"You are worthy, our Lord and God, to receive glory and honor and power, for You created all things, and by Your will they were created and have their being."
Revelation 4:11

BIBLIOGRAPHY

Armstrong, Thomas. *In Their Own Way.* Jeremy P. Tarcher, Inc.

Arndt, Elise. *A Mother's Time.* Victor Books.

Aslett, Don. *Clutter's Last Stand.* Writer's Digest Books.

Berman, Eleanor. "Get Control of Clutter" in *Working Mother* magazine.

Bradshaw, John. *Creating Love.* Bantam.

Buck, Pearl S. *To My Daughters With Love.* John Day, Publishers.

Chapman, Annie. *Smart Women Keep It Simple.* Bethany House.

Culp, Stephanie. *How to Conquer Clutter.* Writer's Digest Books.

Dayton, Edward & Engstrom, Ted. *Strategy for Living.* Gospel Light.

Elkind, David. T*he Hurried Child.* Addison-Wesley Publishing Co.

Fanning, Tony & Robbie. *Get It All Done and Still Be Human.* Chilton.

Froehlic, D. Mary Ann. *What's a Smart Woman Like You Doing In a Place Like This?* Wolgemuth & Hyatt Publishers.

Gillie, Paul. "Trend Toward Simple Life Just Keeps Growing". *Kalamazoo Gazette.*

Hunter, Brenda. *Home by Choice: Facing the Affects of a Mother's Absence.* Penguin.

Jenks, James & Kelly, John. *Don't Do, Delegate!* Franklin Watts.

Mackenzie, Alex. *The Time Trap.* American Management Assoc.

McBride, Pat. *How to Get Your Act Together.* Thomas Nelson, Pubs.

McCullough, Bonnie & Mason, Susan. *101 Ways to Get Your Kids to Work at Home.* St. Martin's Press

McDonald, Gordon. *Ordering Your Private World.* Thomas Nelson.

Menzel, Peter. *Material World.* Sierra Club Books.

Minirth & Meier. *We Are Driven - The Compulsive Behavior America Applauds.* Guideposts.

Minton, Michael. *What Is a Wife Worth?* McGraw-Hill.

Osborn, Carol. *Enough Is Enough.* G.P. Putnam, Sons.

Perry Susan & Dawson, Jim. *The Secrets our Body Clocks Reveal.* Ballantine Books.

Schofield, Deniece. *Confessions of an Organized Housewife.* Writer's Digest Books.

Scripture verses - all versions, mostly KJV, NKJV, NIV, Living NT.

Spring, Beth. "Having It All At Home." *Focus on the Family* magazine.

Stautberg, Susan & Worthing, Marcia. *Balancing Acts.* MasterMedia Ltd.

Stronach, Rena. *How to take the Hassle Out of Home Making.* Living Books.

Thompson, John. "Replacing Passive Rebellion with Biblical Motivation". *Teaching Home.*

Wheeler, Bonnie. *The Hurrier I Go.* Regal Books

A special thank you to my son, Sam Morrison, for all of his help!

ABOUT THE AUTHOR

Dawn Ulmer, by her own admission, has made most of the mistakes hurried woman make while trying to manage a career and raise a family. Through those mistakes she's learned valuable life lessons that she's been imparting to other women both in writing and in workshop presentations. She especially enjoyed sharing her knowledge in a time management column for a regional magazine for women. This book is the culmination of her experiences and research. Dawn is clearly passionate about helping women live balanced lives. As a result, she also created and moderates the Balance for the Hurried Woman site on Facebook where women can find encouragement and advice.

You are welcome to correspond with Dawn through email, or you can also join the Facebook Group, Balance for the Hurried Woman.

hurriedwomen@gmail.com

https://www.facebook.com/groups/BalanceForTheHurriedWoman/

Made in the USA
San Bernardino, CA
15 April 2018